Leaders Behaving Badly

LEADERS BEHAVING BADLY

What happens when ordinary people show up, stand up and speak up

Ann Andrews CSP

Activity Press

Published by Activity Press

Contact author: www.annandrews.co.nz

A catalogue record for this book is available from the National Library of New Zealand.

To our much-loved grandson Blair
(9 September 2003 – 9 March 2018)

Soccer hero, computer whiz,
leader-in-waiting

Gone way too soon

CONTENTS

Introduction 1

Chapter information 3

I. The leadership enigma

1. What type of leader are you? 11
   - *Above-the-line leadership* 11
   - *Accidental and/or reluctant leaders* 15
   - *Healthy disruption versus dysfunctional chaos* 17
   - *Do women make better leaders than men?* 19
2. Why leaders fear making mistakes 23
   - *We've always done it that way* 23
   - *Decision-making in real time* 26
   - *Why changing what you don't understand is far worse than making a mistake* 27
   - *Balancing fresh thinking with zero experience* 28
   - *Reputations are on the line every day* 28
3. Tough leader or bully? 30
   - *Below-the-line leadership* 30
   - *The difference between harassment and bullying* 31
   - *What bullying is and what it isn't* 32
   - *The staggering costs of bullying* 34
   - *Sooner or later bullies meet their Waterloo* 35
4. Owning the culture and naming the games 37
   - *Creating the culture of an organisation* 37
   - *Understanding the power of 'values'* 38
   - *The delusional games some leaders play* 39
   - *Children are master game players* 42
   - *Naming the games* 42
   - *The danger of normalising bad behaviour* 43
   - *The entitlement syndrome* 44
   - *At what point does behaviour cross a line?* 45

5. Understanding the enablers 48

The fatal attraction between people who display bad behaviours and the people who enable them 48

Why do people support and even encourage such obvious bad behaviour? 50

Taking the 'pledge' 52

Leaker or whistle-blower? 53

All hail the incredible courage of whistle-blowers 54

The cost of turning a blind eye 57

II. Politicians behaving badly

6. Power given can just as easily be taken away 61

Did that really just happen? 61

Politics and politicians 63

Do politicians have a responsibility to be ethical? 64

Dirty tactics 64

When in danger of being caught out, deny, distract, denigrate and divert attention 67

Alternative facts, and fake news 69

Does power make smart people do really dumb things? 70

Leaders who don't listen to sage advice or study history are destined to repeat the same mistakes 71

Mud sticks; how dirty tactics brought Hillary Clinton down 73

III. Presidents behaving badly

7. The power of profiling 79

The truth is never about what you say, it's about what you do, and that's always about who you are 79

The very dark side of leadership 84

A duty to warn 85

8. The Trump effect 88

The Trump personality: brilliant, dangerous or just plain old sad? 88

President versus presidency 89

Games Trump plays 90

Be careful what you wish for, you may just get it 94

Learned behaviours 94

We are the sum total of everything we believe about ourselves 96

The ripple effects of his presidency 97

Why he lies and the damage that causes 99

Past behaviours usually predict future behaviours 103

Why could voters not see through him? 104

The eight key areas where Trump is literally carving out the heart and soul of America 106

Is his 'Make America Great Again' slogan really a covert plan to make America white again? 115

Has he amassed a following or has he actually created a cult? 117

Is he making America irrelevant on the global stage? 117

Is Trump himself being 'played'? 120

Will he be remembered as a leader, a would-be dictator or a martyr? 122

IV. Leaders and politicians behaving naively

9. Our future really is coming, ready or not 127

Facebook made to face facts 127

Turning a blind eye to the clear warnings 130

Failure to ask 'What if?' 131

Learning on the run 132

Truth will rise to the surface (eventually) 132

10. If not me, then who? 134

Do we get the leaders we deserve? 134

Why aren't young people voting? 135

Understanding followership 137

The responsibilities of followers 139

Some people are standing up to him 140

11. Leaders behaving consciously 142

Are you a conscious leader? 142

The paradox of being a good leader in one area and a poor leader in another 144

Knowing when your time has come 145

Knowing when your time has gone 146

Understanding life after the spotlight and the art of giving back 147

When you see an opportunity to make a difference, take it 148

V. A thirst for change

12. The planet is crying out for leaders to play the long game 153

Short-term gratification versus long-term regret 153

The urgent need for leaders to become futurists 154

The cost of ignoring early warning signs 155

Factoring in costs versus benefits 155

Water: the gold of the future? 156

Mining madness 158

Breathe in, breathe out 160

The plastic dilemma 160

Some messes may be impossible to clean up 161

Our future is coming, ready or not 161

13. The fightback has begun 162

A giant wake-up call 162

When you see an opportunity to make a difference, don't miss the moment 164

The women's movement is reborn 164

Name and shame movements rising to the surface 168

The climate change movement gathers momentum 169

The great news 170

The amazing news 171

How a 'Youthquake' is showing up apathetic leaders 173

The only way is up 174

VI. The Fourth Wave

14. Global challenges need global solutions 179

The Third Wave 179

So many problems, so many ways to avoid facing them 181

Technology: our greatest weapon, our greatest fear 183

The crisis of trust 185

Finding a way to deal with the tyrants and despots 186

Championing civility and kinder politics 188

15. Don't give up on democracy 190

Kia kaha, people everywhere 193

Recommended reading 195

Further resources 197

Further reading 198

Acknowledgements 199

About the author 201

Other books by the author 206

References 208

INTRODUCTION

When I finished writing the 'Trump' book (*Lessons in Leadership*: 50 ways to avoid falling into the Trump trap) I thought that was it. I'd done it. I'd said my piece. I'd said Trump's behaviours were not okay. I'd offered some alternative behaviours for leaders and potential leaders to follow rather than thinking that if it was okay for the President of the USA to marginalise and abuse people, then it must be okay for others to treat people that way. It isn't!

Even after I'd closed the book off (albeit with the words 'To be continued'), I really thought he couldn't get any worse, and then every day he did.

He seemed to have no ability or desire to learn on the job or to improve his communication skills. It was clear that his modus operandi would be to keep on endlessly blaming others for mistakes he was making and I watched in never-ending horror as his name-calling, fabrications and highly dangerous tweeting continued unabated.

It became more obvious by the day that he had no concept of the right thing to do in any given situation, in fact if there was a right way or a wrong way to do something, it seemed that he would most likely choose the wrong way even when choosing the right way was possibly even simpler.

Leaders should model good behaviour. They should be above name-calling and blaming and throwing people under buses. Sadly, Donald Trump isn't. So I will keep on writing because I fear his 'normalising' bad behaviours, not only in other politicians but in other leaders, in communities, in schools, in families and in children.

We have an acknowledged global online bullying problem, so

doing what he does via Twitter gives permission to the kids who are likely to bully others online. It's fairly logical for people who have a tendency to bullying to think it must be okay if the President of the USA gets away with doing it on a daily basis.

When people ask, 'Who are you and why do you think you are qualified to make comments on the President of the USA?', my reply is this: in my book, seeing that something is horribly wrong and speaking up is far better than the bigger sin of seeing something wrong and turning a blind eye. And we don't need an alphabet soup of letters after our names to see that what Trump is doing is a million miles away from being okay.

I also believe there are two groups of people who can and should ask awkward questions:

Young children when they ask us 'Why?' and we adults can't find a logical answer because we've been found wanting

Grandmothers who have been around the block a few times, who've seen the best of behaviours and the worst of behaviours and have no problem calling out those bad behaviours no matter who is displaying them. I fit into the grandmother category and so as long as Donald keeps displaying his totally inappropriate and even dangerous behaviours, I'll keep calling them out.

I keep hoping and praying that he won't last much longer as POTUS. I keep hoping and praying that, at best, he will work out that he is out of his depth and graciously resign, though that is probably wishful thinking, or he will be impeached or even that the 25th Amendment will be invoked.

I live in hope.

> *'Capitalism is the extraordinary belief that the nastiest of men for the nastiest of motives will somehow work for the benefit of all.'*
> — John Maynard Keynes

CHAPTER INFORMATION

In the interim or even in the aftermath of any of those things happening, I want to look at the bigger issues the world is facing:

- Democracies versus dictatorships
- Political systems that don't seem to serve the people
- The sheer waste of money in the political arena because of partisan behaviour

The simple idea that politicians should be working together on issues rather than turning everything they touch into political footballs. Incredibly important topics like health and education and feeding an ever-growing human population and looking after an aging population and perhaps tackling global warming; just a few of the tough challenges on our horizon.

I also want to ponder what I hope and pray is a 'sea change' in politics. I want to explore what happened here in New Zealand politics in our elections. Yes, we are a small country and in no way could our challenges measure up against the challenges of the USA; however, we have witnessed a different kind of politician emerging and causing a stir. I want to talk about 'kinder' politics and the potential of what that could do to encourage younger people to not only get out and use their votes, but perhaps to become more involved in the political sphere. After all, it is their future that is on the line if we don't change the current political systems.

If we keep witnessing kindergarten behaviours from people who should know better and should behave more professionally and we keep accepting those abysmal standards, then we probably get the leaders we deserve.

Part 1 of the book focuses on the complex and confusing leadership enigma.

In Chapter 1 I ask, 'What type of leader are you?' I discuss leadership per se and the types of leadership styles and skills I've met over my years in HR. I discuss what happens when people become accidental and even reluctant leaders; people who see something that isn't right and step up to bring about change. I talk about healthy change versus dysfunctional chaos and how to tell the difference and I use current research to analyse whether women make better leaders than men.

In Chapter 2 I look at why leaders fear making mistakes and why it is often easier to just do things the way they've always been done because that feels safer and the outcome is more predictable. I also share my thoughts on why changing something a leader doesn't understand is actually worse than making a mistake. I look at finding the balance between bringing on board people with fresh ideas and energy but with little or no experience. And I look at how reputations can be lost in the blink of an eye if solid foundations are not built or are forgotten or even neglected.

Chapter 3 asks the question 'Tough leader or bully?' and explores the dark side of people in power. I look at the difference between harassment and bullying; what bullying is and what it isn't. I also share some of the costs of bullying, in monetary terms, but also in terms of the health and wellbeing of the targets of a bully.

Chapter 4 discusses the culture of organisations, how culture is created and what it is built on. I also introduce the things that destroy culture; the games people play because of vested interest or because they are recruited into positions which are simply beyond them but they fear the humiliation of admitting that they are way out of their depth. I talk about the dangers of normalising poor behaviour and that organisations and leaders need to be very clear which behaviours cross a line.

Chapter 5 I've dedicated to the 'enablers' of poor behaviour. I want to help the reader understand the mysterious attraction between leaders who behave badly and the people around them who make that poor behaviour okay. I share a case study of a hospital that designed a process to stamp out bad behaviour and encouraged people to speak up. I discuss the difference between a leaker and a whistle-blower and share some courageous examples of people who risked all manner of retribution by alerting the outside world to poor behaviours. And I share some of the costs to organisations that preferred to turn a blind eye.

Part 2 of the book focuses on politicians behaving badly.

In Chapter 6 I highlight the recent introduction of dirty tactics, alternative facts and fake news into our daily lives. I researched whether power makes people do really dumb things, and discovered that it does. I share the story of how dirty tactics changed the face of American politics.

Part 3 of the book looks at presidents behaving badly.

Chapter 7 is dedicated to understanding the power of profiling a person before you recruit them so you don't fall into the trap of putting them into a position they may be unsuitable for. I discuss the darkness of leadership and the concern 27 psychiatrists raised when they feared that Donald Trump could potentially become President of the USA.

Chapter 8 is dedicated to trying, in some small way, to understand Donald Trump. I ask the question 'Is he brilliant, dangerous or just plain sad?' I discuss the confusion between the role of president versus the respect that traditionally goes with the office of the presidency. I discuss the games that Trump plays on a daily and even hourly basis; how he thrives on chaos. I discuss the effect this has on the people around him; why they will constantly disappoint him and why he will inevitably end up throwing them under a bus; sometimes within a matter of days of joining his team. I talk about learned behaviours; how past behaviours pretty much predict future behaviours. I wonder why people couldn't see through him on the campaign trail and why the GOP fails to call him out. And I ponder the long-term effects on America and the world as a result of his presidency.

Part 4 of the book focuses on leaders and politicians behaving naively.

Chapter 9 explores the Facebook melt down, when allegedly Russians used Facebook to interfere and distort the results of the 2016 American election. This interference spiralled into the firing of James Comey, then FBI director, and the resultant setting up of a Special Council headed by Robert Mueller to investigate Russian interference. Facebook is a modern example of how things can go horribly wrong and not only destroy reputations overnight, but actually result in the demise of previously successful businesses. I explore a very young leader, Mark Zuckerberg, successfully launching a business that had no predecessor; they literally had to design and make decisions on the run. On the surface they had a business that ran smoothly and effectively, but suddenly it was exposed as having some gaping flaws and questionable values, which were easily exploited by a rogue element.

Chapter 10 moves to looking at followership. I ask the question 'Do we get the leaders we deserve?' I also ask why young people are not voting. I expand on the responsibilities of 'followership' in a world where it is too easy to blame someone else for our personal misfortunes.

In Chapter 11 I explore leaders behaving consciously. Why leaders need to realise that they can be great leaders in one area and in one time, but terrible leaders in different circumstances. I talk about the need for leaders to know when their time has come but equally to be aware when their time has gone. I also discuss the tough yet exciting realisation when they realise that there is life after the spotlight.

Part 5 of the book is about a thirst for change on a global level.

Chapter 12 stresses the need for leaders and politicians to start playing a long game; to stop looking for short-terms gains at the expense of long-term costs in whatever way those costs pan out. I discuss the dangers of ignoring early warning signs of all manner of potential disasters. I look at the abuse of waterways through extensive farming and unsafe manufacturing and mining practices. I compare various cities around the world where their water is so polluted it is undrinkable and their air is so toxic it is killing millions of people per year.

In Chapter 13 I look at the groundswell of new leaders that are rising to challenge outdated thinking and unacceptable behaviours. I discuss the women's #MeToo movement; the name and shame efforts around the world calling out corporates behaving badly. I look at the massive climate change leadership coming, not from the establishment but from all manner of unusual places. I share some great news, some amazing news and how a 'Youthquake' is showing up apathetic leaders in ways they simply cannot avoid or shy away from.

Part 6 of the book shares the emergence of what I'll call the Fourth Wave.

In Chapter 14 I discuss Alvin Toffler's concept of the Third Wave, which, I think, lays the platform for understanding where we need to go as a global community if we want seven billion people on this planet to survive. I talk about the fact that the enormous global challenges we are facing actually do need global solutions, and I fear that the lack of trust in our current leaders is dividing us all rather than uniting us, not just in communities but in and between countries. I address the fear people have that technology is taking away their jobs but the advantages it could bring if we choose to embrace it and make it work for us rather than against us. I share my thoughts on the need for leaders to champion civility and kindness in politics because if our leaders act this way, then our kids will have great role models and they too will be more civil and kind and everything else in their lives will flow from that.

In Chapter 15 I urge us not to give up on democracy. I discuss the challenges democracy brings, but offer the thought that the opposite is simply not an alternative we would ever want, that we need to fight for democracy as individuals, as families, as communities and as countries.

PART I

THE LEADERSHIP ENIGMA

'I'm not afraid of an army of lions led by a sheep, I'm afraid of an army of sheep led by a lion.'
— Alexander the Great

1

WHAT TYPE OF LEADER ARE YOU?

'Until you make peace with who you are, you'll never be content with what you have.'
— Doris Mortman

Above-the-line leadership

Being a parent is probably the hardest job any of us will ever take on. No matter how many books we read or how many workshops we attend, our children defy all books and workshops; we have to learn how to parent *them,* to understand their personality types, their unique needs and wants.

Becoming a leader is probably the second hardest job in the world.

As owners or managers, supervisors or team leaders, we will have good days and bad days. We will have days when no matter what happens around us we are able to remain calm and logical and decisive. And then we will have days where everything that can possibly go wrong, does. The alarm clock doesn't go off. We get stuck in horrendous traffic. We run out of petrol on the way to work. We get caught in a torrential downpour on the way from the car park to the office. Whatever. We are only human. If we've had a start to our day along those lines, we probably won't be calm and logical and decisive. We will be short-tempered, irrational and indecisive. We are only human.

However, no matter the type of day we are having, I've noticed over my years in HR that there are some basic leadership styles that lie underneath whatever is going on for us; a good day or a bad day may be temporary, but our personalities and styles are pretty fixed.

The most well-known leadership styles are as follows:

- Autocratic: the get-things-done boss. These people on their bad day could resort to the 'my-way-or-the-highway' style of decision-making. Even on a normal day, if results don't come fast enough, they will not be happy and people around them will be left in no doubt that they are not happy.
- Democratic: leaders who involve their people, ask for their ideas, include them in decision-making. Though they too are only human. They too could resort to becoming autocratic if they feel that things are becoming too cruisy.
- Laissez faire: leaders who tend to sit back or even hide in their office appearing to take little or no interest in what is happening with their people. If they are having a bad day, they will probably put up a 'Do Not Disturb' notice and be even more unavailable.

My belief has always been that on a normal, rational day, a leader needs to know how to combine all three — a 'know-when-to-hold-'em and know-when-to-fold-'em' style. In other words, know when to step in and take charge (autocratic); know when to step back and let people get on with things (laissez faire), and know when involvement and inclusion are required (democratic).

None of us is one-dimensional; there are other styles that are woven into the fabric of who a leader is and how and where he or she will perform best:

- The charismatic leader: someone who has an abundance of charm and personality. This is a person who naturally attracts people with his or her sheer passion and personality. This could be a democratic leader with personality, and even an autocratic leader with a touch of pizzazz.
- The visionary leader: someone who has a clear picture in mind of what the future looks like and can paint that picture so others will be inspired by it and join him or her on the journey.
- The strategic leader: a person with the skills required in a start-up or new team. Someone who has the big picture clearly in mind and will take a new team or group along with him or her confidently during the early stages of a business.
- The transitional leader: required when a business has sudden growth or takes over another business. A person who has a steady hand and doesn't panic easily. A person who has the long game in mind.
- The situational/facilitative leader: someone who can coordinate the people, processes and skills required at a particular time in the life cycle of a business. Someone who can bring those different factions together and help them find a way through to consensus and a desired outcome.
- The operational leader: someone who can literally step in, become hands on if need be to get things happening, get things moving. He or she can clearly see the challenges and can implement systems to smooth out operational road blocks.

Most of us are a mix of many of them.

These leadership styles are all what I would define as 'above-the-line' leadership styles. They are genuine; they are authentic; the style may not be perfect but there is no ill intent involved. Each 'style' may be a challenge for an organisation in that it has recruited the wrong style for a given scenario; however, what is *not* in question here are the 'ethics' of each style.

Which leadership 'type' feels like you; which resonates with you? If you are not 100% happy with your leadership style, or if perhaps you realise you are not getting the results you were employed to achieve, can you change?

I believe that about 80–90% of who we are is pretty much set in stone at birth. If I'm a quiet introvert, I will never be a life-and-soul-of-the-party person. If I'm a get-things-done person, I will have to be seriously disciplined not to take over from people if I don't think they are moving fast enough.

However, knowing our strengths and weaknesses goes a long way to changing what we can about our personality or recruiting the people around us that offer the balance.

- What type of leader do you aspire to be?
- Who do you hold up as your role model?

Malala Yousafzai, the young Muslim girl shot by the Taliban for going to school, said, 'One book, one pen, one child and one teacher can change the world.' And so it is with a leader; leaders can literally change the world around them for better or for worse.

Consider some of the 'greats':

- Gandhi had a vision to peacefully rid India of Western powers — a movement that became known as Enlightened Anarchy.

- Lincoln was determined to end slavery in America.
- Mandela was determined to end apartheid.
- Kennedy set a goal of a man on the moon by the end of the 1980s when no-one had the technology to do so.
- Martin Luther King Jr wanted to end racial prejudice.
- Mother Teresa founded a nunnery dedicated to helping the poor and the sick in India.

Did they all have the same leadership style? Absolutely not. Did each of them have good days and bad days? Of course they did. Were they logical and rational one day and grumpy another? Probably.

But to a man and woman, they had their long-term goals so that even on a really bad day, they would look beyond personal challenges and moods to stay on track with their vision. Was their vision achieved easily and without effort? Absolutely not. Did they take one step forward and numerous steps back? Of course they did. Their strategies were probably designed on the run. Did they make mistakes? Undoubtedly. But their goal or vision was such that no roadblock was ever going to stop them.

Some people choose leadership, while others came by their leadership role totally by default.

Accidental and/or reluctant leaders

On 1 December 1955, in Montgomery, Alabama, Rosa Parks refused to give up her seat to a white man when the 'white' section of the bus was full. She eventually became involved with the civil rights movement of that period, even collaborating with Martin Luther King Jr, who at that stage in history was a new minister in town. She decided that she was 'tired of giving in'.

Tarana Burke said, 'You have to use your privilege to serve other people.' In October 2017, Burke, who at that stage had 500 Twitter followers, picked up the news that Harvey Weinstein had been named by the *New York Times* as a sexual abuser. Burke worked with survivors of sexual abuse and had called her group 'Me Too', at best hoping that the phrase might become a bumper sticker to encourage other victims to seek help. Now suddenly her 'Me Too' slogan had been used over 12 million times because Alyssa Milano, American actress, activist, producer and former singer, had innocently picked up the phrase and turned it into the now-famous #MeToo phrase.

A movement was born.

Rosa Parks and Tarana Burke — and even Alyssa Milano — became accidental and possibly even reluctant leaders. All of them had simply reached the end of the road of what they felt was tolerable. Each in their own way said, 'Enough.'

And that actually sums up good leadership.

Mother Teresa was once asked if she would join a march against war; she declined, however she said she would be happy to join a march *for* peace.

Leaders need to know what they stand for and be really clear about the lines they will not cross. They need to be so passionate and determined to achieve their vision or goal that no matter what, they will stand their ground without ever going against their own moral compass, because if leaders are sure-footed and clear, their followers will be sure-footed and clear.

The absolute base camp of leadership is to know exactly where you are going, and to be willing to do whatever it takes to get there. To never lose faith; to never compromise your values; to totally believe in your dream and the willingness to take people with you; and to never do anything that fouls your message.

> *'Never let yourself be persuaded that any one Great Man, any one leader, is necessary to the salvation of America. When America consists of one leader and 158 million followers, it will no longer be*

America.'
— Dwight D. Eisenhower

Healthy disruption versus dysfunctional chaos

Virtually every organisation or team I've worked with over the years employed me to help them change some aspect of their team or organisation.

Whether it was to deal with a high absenteeism problem, a high turnover of skilled talent or simply the need to be more profitable — all were situations that required an intervention or change of current practices so that the issues were addressed and solutions uncovered.

Change ruffles feathers. I read somewhere that it isn't that people hate change, it's that they hate *being* changed.

Some change is healthy and necessary. People who love current systems are usually people who benefit from the status quo; they are also the people who will resist any changes with every fibre of their being. In business and careers, stagnation is not healthy. Businesses go out of business, and people who don't upskill end up on the scrapheap.

Change may require a company to disband certain unprofitable product lines or services, which in turn could lead to loss of jobs. There will absolutely be times when such tough decisions have to be made in order for the business as a whole to survive.

High absenteeism is often the result of a poor manager; people who report to the manager feel under-valued, not included, not listened to. If we investigate high turnover, we will find that people aren't leaving the organisation, they are leaving a poor manager.

And so organisations needs systems and processes in place that are able to deal with poor managers; another of those situations that may require tough decisions to be made: retrain or remove poor managers?

Rosa Parks, Tarana Burke and Alyssa Milano were all 'change agents' — they stood up for something and against something else. I have absolutely no doubt that many people will hate what these three women unleashed.

Dysfunctional chaos is a whole different story. Leaders who decide to change things for the sake of making a personal mark regardless of the cost are actually the worst kind of leaders.

I have to use Donald Trump as my example here — I will come back to Trump in much more detail later but for the sake of addressing leaders who want to change something simply to make a mark, there is no better example at the moment.

Trump campaigned on 'draining the swamp'; he tapped into the belief among many people that the American government was clumsy, expensive and didn't serve the American people. Wanting to improve that system would have been a 'healthy' change. However, destroying every part of the system, setting various departments of the American system up against each other, seeding distrust, polarising every aspect of the system and creating an ever bigger and more insidious swamp can only do damage that will take years to heal and will be costing the American public long after Trump ceases to be President.

Any leader worth his or her salt, particularly a leader going into a completely different sector, would take time to investigate systems, to find out why the systems were there in the first place. He or she would take time to speak to every single departmental head to find out more about them and how their departments functioned. Then and only then would he or she consider what changes needed to be made to have a better-functioning operation.

Of course, a leader wants to make a mark, to have it make a

difference that they were there at all; but simply trashing and burning everything and everybody all at the one time just to make themselves look tough and all powerful is a recipe for certain disaster.

Do women make better leaders than men?

Throughout the world, whether in business or in government, most of our leaders are men. Right now we have our fair share of despots, but throughout the ages there have always been despots.

I'm not a man so I don't know how 'tough' it is to be a man. I'm sure they have their stresses and grievances also; I'm sure they must feel undervalued and taken for granted at times.

I remember once attending a personal growth gathering of men and women, when a male speaker asked us all to think about what our fathers would have done differently with their lives if they hadn't had to support a family. And the room went very quiet. That question hit all of us quite deeply. Because our fathers and grandfathers did bear burdens for their families. They fought in wars; they probably also worked in jobs they hated just to put food on the table. Many of them probably also worked for ungrateful bosses. They too probably felt harassed and bullied at times.

So this isn't meant to be a put-down of the good male leaders of which there are many, but in an article in *Harvard Business Review* by Jack Zenger, CEO, and Joseph Folkman, President, of Zenger Folkman, a leadership development consultancy, they quote their survey of 7280 leaders they evaluated in 2011. The study confirmed some 'truths about men and women leaders in the workplace but also holds some surprises'.

They surveyed leaders in successful and progressive organisations in the public and private arena; in government and commercial organisations both domestic and international. They asked for comparisons between male and female leaders from peers, bosses, direct reports and other associates.

At all levels women rated higher than men in virtually all of the 16 competencies Zenger and Folkman had defined as the competencies for success. In fact, men outscored women in only one area — the ability to develop a strategic perspective. In other areas such as 'takes initiative; practices self-development; displays high integrity and honesty; drives for results; develops others', women outperformed their male counterparts.

Zenger and Folkman then went on to share their findings with a group of women outside the survey, asking them why they thought women had rated this way. The responses were:

'We need to work harder than men to prove ourselves.'

'We feel the constant pressure to never make a mistake, and to continually prove our value to the organization.'

And to further stress that expectations of women in leadership are tougher for women, ECI (Ethics and Compliance Initiative) conducted a study to find out how male and female leaders are committed to ethics in their workplace.

They discovered from the survey results that men and women 'are about equally committed to ethics in the workplace, but female leaders face much greater ethics risks than male counterparts.' That:

- women in senior leadership positions are more likely than men at the same level to feel pressure to compromise company ethics standards and/or the law,
- women are more likely to experience retaliation for reporting misconduct, and
- women are more likely to doubt their leaders' commitment to workplace integrity.

I'd just finished reading Hillary Clinton's *What Happened* because I simply couldn't believe that she was beaten in the recent presidential run. She won every debate hands down, and yet as I watched those various debates I remembered thinking that she said one controversial thing when she used the phrase 'basket of deplorables' and was berated up hill and down dale for it. Yet at every opportunity Trump was doing his name-calling and belittling of everyone he met including a handicapped journalist and no-one, it appears, told Donald that this was absolutely not okay. Imagine if Hillary had created some form of chant about Trump that had audiences berating and ridiculing him. How would he and his supporters have handled that?

But that wasn't her way.

She made one mistake with her emails, which she acknowledged and which led to the famous 'Lock her up!' chant. Trump still tweets every day on an unsafe android phone and continues to break every norm and every rule in the book without a murmur from his voters or the GOP.

Clinton says that she has a sign in her house that says:

> *It's hard to be a woman.*
> *You must think like a man,*
> *Act like a lady,*
> *Look like a young girl,*
> *And work like a horse.*

In my own experience, I've met great leaders of both genders, and similarly I've met terrible leaders of both genders.

Perhaps it stands out more if a woman behaves badly, or perhaps society treats women more harshly or expects more of them. Perhaps when there are more women in leadership we won't stand out so much and perhaps then we will be taken seriously. Perhaps then we will take the mess the world is currently in and straighten it out so that there is a planet left for our daughters and grand-daughters to inherit.

> *'Some leaders are born women.'*
> — Geraldine Ferrero

2

WHY LEADERS FEAR MAKING MISTAKES

'Any man can make a mistake but only an idiot persists in his error.'
— Cicero

We've always done it that way

If you've ever started work in a new organisation and wondered why they do things a certain way, and if you then venture to courageously ask, you will be told, 'We've always done it that way.' Organisations do what they do in a certain way because it usually means they won't make any mistakes; it is a proven way, it is safe, it is tried and true. The downside of that way of thinking is that they won't make any improvements either.

I'm familiar with businesses offering this strategy, but after watching the election of Donald Trump, I fear politics and politicians seem to fall into the same trap.

I was born in the UK and lived there until my mid-twenties. I had a stepfather who was very involved in what was then the UK Liberal Party, so we had lots of political people at the house and I'd sit on the fringes of lots of political discussions.

What I didn't realise at the time was that I was actually absorbing 'liberal' ideas, and I know that to be called a liberal in the USA seems to be tantamount to being called 'pond scum', which is interesting, because the dictionary definition of liberal thinking is 'generous, open minded, of political party favouring democratic reforms'. I'm really cool with that explanation and happy to choose it as my basic value system.

My then husband and I along with our two young children emigrated to New Zealand in the early 1970s to a much smaller political scene. There were two dominant parties — Labour and National — and two smaller parties — Social Credit and the Values Party. My immediate affinity was with the Values Party.

I've always voted. I am of the generation that knew full well what women had gone through to get votes for women, and I was immensely proud to learn that New Zealand was the first country in the world to give women the vote.

However, the political debates I'd witnessed in the UK, New Zealand and America over the years followed a similar pattern. Rubbish the opposition; use put-downs, innuendo and fear tactics to make the other party look bad. And when in doubt, blame, blame, blame.

And so parliaments look like kindergartens, with grown adults hurling insults across the divide. And I'd never liked that.

Since the election of Trump, trashing the opposition took a darker and more sinister turn. Ridiculing the opposition no longer seemed to be enough, and so began a new era of politics — the emergence of fake news, alternative facts and dirty tactics.

The year 2017 was one of the most chaotic I can remember in my lifetime, and I'm no longer a young thing. It felt as if the whole world had gone mad; that we had either become 'bit' players in a living soap opera or possibly even strayed into an alternative universe.

No-one likes making mistakes. We feel dumb and stupid when we do. But it's crazy to think that we will never make mistakes. Just think back to learning to ride a bike or learning to roller-skate. Of course we will fall over; of course we get skinned knees, of course we look and feel stupid. But do we give up learning? Of course we don't. We get up and try again, and again and again until we master whatever it is.

The worst things about making mistakes is not acknowledging it; not learning from it or worst of all blaming someone else for the mistake.

I know from experience that a classic mistake in many organisations is to promote some bright person into a management position and to be told to 'go manage'. He or she receives no training, no coach, no mentor, and the promotion becomes sink or swim. And sadly, a lot of newly promoted managers and team leaders do sink.

The problem for leaders of large companies, politicians or even country leaders is that their mistakes are literally there for all the world to see and could even appear as headlines in a news report or on TV. A goof or a gaffe, a throwaway remark, a joke that went awry, or a drink too many near a camera or smartphone and their mistakes can go viral within minutes.

Who can ever forget Tony Hayward, then CEO of BP, saying 'I want my life back' after the Deepwater oil rig explosion? Eleven workers were killed and the explosion caused the worst oil spill in US history. His insensitive comments went viral within hours.

Making mistakes makes leaders seem incompetent or weak or

disorganised or out of their depth. And once opposition parties get involved to inflame a mistake, then careers are on the line.

So as a leader, what to do?

If you've made a mistake, admit it: own it and do that quickly. But then don't make that same mistake again. Involve people you respect before you make a decision. Talk to people with experience; ask for advice; listen and learn. Become a reader of history — there are very few mistakes that haven't already been made by someone before you. The leader that isn't willing to learn, simply won't be a leader for very long.

Decision-making in real time

The whole world witnessed a couple of massive mistakes in 2017.

Theresa May and the Brexit vote. Mrs May announced a surprise call for an election when she already held a massive majority in the UK Parliament. Her rationale was that she wanted to strengthen her stand in Brexit negotiations.

I'm sure she fully expected that people would want to remain in the EU, but by a slim majority the 'leave' voters won the day. Panic ensued across Britain, across Europe and probably across the world. Share markets crashed as people moved into safer financial havens, and the British pound experienced the biggest single-day fall since the Second World War.

Two years on, it doesn't appear that much has improved. According to Timothy Garten Ash writing for the *Guardian*, 'the Brits can't agree what they want' and he goes on to say that 'it's painful to see Britain in such a shambolic mess.'

Britain has seen many upheavals over the last few hundred years and I'm sure it will survive — whether Theresa May will survive her decision is another matter.

James Comey's handling of the Hillary Clinton email saga. In an article in the *Washington Post,* Aaron Blake labelled Comey's decision to disclose that the FBI was reviewing more of Hillary Clinton's emails 'unavoidably horrible'. Coming just 11 days before the American presidential election, this announcement by Comey has been blamed by many people, including Clinton herself, for her narrow loss to Donald Trump.

The ramifications of both these decisions will reverberate for many years, both internally to each country, but globally as well. It will take several years for Britain to uncouple from the EU with all the confusion that goes along with the negotiations; and having Donald Trump as POTUS is already causing massive disruption across the globe in ways no-one could have predicted.

Did the Electoral College make a massive mistake in 2017 when they overturned the popular vote in favour of Hillary becoming POTUS and instead unleashed Donald Trump on the world?

Why changing what you don't understand is far worse than making a mistake

The opposite side of 'We've always done it that way' is that sometimes things are done that way for a very good reason.

Leaders are placed in a dilemma the second they take on a new role. They are expected to make an instant impression but at this stage they probably don't know the best places to start. This is where a good leader will gather all his or her people together and encourage a free and open discussion of where they think changes need to be made. Doing this kills several birds with one stone: it says you are listening and that you care; it says that you want to help your people with their challenges; but it also says that you are serious about making whatever improvements are required to help the business or country as a whole.

Balancing fresh thinking with zero experience

Every new leader wants to surround himself or herself with people he or she knows and trusts. Taking on a new role where you know none of the people who will report to you means just that — you don't know them; you don't know who supports your appointment or who resents it. The easiest solution is to bring in all your own people; however, it also means that you risk losing the vast experience that resides in the existing team.

This is another scenario where it is advisable to take time, get to know people, get to know the problems, set some things in motion, test the results and then and only then consider bringing in some of your own people. The very worst thing a new leader can do is to get rid of everyone at the one time and replace them with his or her own people.

Changing things for the sake of changing them is a no-win. Changing what you don't understand is also a no-win and an even bigger mistake.

Reputations are on the line every day

If a leader thinks he or she can be one person in public and a different person in private, then he or she is sadly mistaken. In a world where videos go viral and tweets get shared with millions within hours, it really does behove everyone in the public arena to have their 's#%t' together, or more politely, to have their 'values' intact. The heat of a situation will show the true 'you' as a leader, just as it will also show the 'truth' of your business.

Johnson & Johnson tarnished its reputation by producing poor quality control Tylenol and Motrin. They further damaged their reputation when they failed to immediately recall the products. Toyota's decision to slacken quality control led to the poor workmanship requiring hundreds of thousands of car recalls.

The company's CEO, Akio Toyoda, was dragged before Congress and chastised for Toyota's apparent lack of concern for safety. The trouble not only hurt the car company's sales, it damaged one of the world's most valuable brands.

CEOs on huge salaries who make poor decisions risk muddying the reputations of their companies for years to come; what damage can country leaders do?

> *'The way to gain a good reputation is to endeavour to be what you desire to appear.'*
> — Socrates

3

TOUGH LEADER OR BULLY?

> *'Most organisations have a serial bully. It never ceases to amaze me how one person's divisive dysfunctional behaviour can permeate the entire organisation like a cancer.'*
> — Tim Field

Below-the-line leadership

I'm sure we've all had a boss who was torture to work for; someone who kept us on edge, who no matter how much we did for them it was never enough. No matter how we did something it was never the 'right' way. No matter how far we went for them it was never far enough.

For example:

- The flip-flop leader who leaves everyone around them confused and exhausted. They want one thing one day and something else the next. They never seem to know what they want; even when you give them what they asked you for, it isn't the right size, shape, proportion or outcome.

- The 'flaky' leader who agrees with one person today and someone else tomorrow.
- The leader who blames everyone else for their mistakes. These are one of the worst leaders to work for because they never take responsibility, never own decisions. These are the type of leader if things go well take the credit but if things go wrong will be missing in action. They are constantly on the lookout for a scapegoat to cover their own bad decisions.
- The 'make-me-look-good' leader. This person is 100% about themselves and 100% not about the people who work for them.
- The 'I-win-you-lose' leader. They will ensure they always win at the other person's expense no matter the long-term consequences.

And then we really go to the depths of the barrel:

- The manipulator. According to *Psychology Today*, most manipulative individuals have four common characteristics:

1. They know how to detect your weaknesses.
2. Once found, they use your weaknesses against you.
3. Through their shrewd machinations, they convince you to give up something of yourself in order to serve their self-centred interests.
4. In work, social and family situations, once a manipulator succeeds in taking advantage of you, he or she will likely repeat the violation until you put a stop to the exploitation.

The difference between harassment and bullying

The harasser. Harassment is usually linked to gender, colour, race, disability and/or a prejudice of some kind. Harassment is obvious. The person being harassed knows immediately that they are being ridiculed because harassers love an audience. Harassers are constantly looking for approval; they love being the centre of attention. Harassment is about bravado, machismo and whatever the female equivalent of machismo is. It's about looking good in front of their mates or co-workers or voters. People who use these tactics often lack self-discipline; they are almost always insecure and are very likely to have personal inadequacies.

The bully. According to Employment New Zealand, workplace bullying is 'repeated and unreasonable behaviour directed towards a worker or a group of workers that can lead to physical or psychological harm. Repeated behaviour is persistent and can involve a range of actions over time.'

The difference is that harassment is almost always done publicly, while bullying, mostly, is done out of sight to ensure there are no witnesses. It then becomes one person's word against the other.

What bullying is and what it isn't

Bullying is about power and control — pure and simple. It is the abuse of position and/or power and it is about actions that are deliberate, debilitating, humiliating and repeated. It is about totally subjugating a person until the bully is certain that person is under their control.

Bullying is also about envy and jealousy, which is why they usually pick 'targets' who are bright and popular; they also pick people who are less likely to fight back. The target may not even realise they are being bullied for quite some time.

Bullies, like harassers, lack in all areas of personal skills. They are totally ignorant of their own behavioural actions and lack any kind of discipline to rein in their actions.

A person can be both a bully and a harasser.

Just as it is important to be able to identify what bullying is, it is equally important to know what bullying is not.

Managers who yell at all their people, who blame everyone, who criticise everything are not necessarily bullies; they may just be miserable people or people who have been promoted way beyond their capabilities and rather than acknowledge that, they make their whole team and everyone around them miserable.

Are men more likely to bully than women?

Most of the surveys done over the years would agree that men are more likely to bully than women, though over the course of my career, I have met a few women who absolutely fall into the category. The Chamber of Commerce of Western Australia discovered that 'Women are more likely to be bullied and experience unwanted sexual advances while men are more likely to be yelled or sworn at'. They also discovered that male-on-male bullying tends to be overt and more apparent to others while women-on-women bullying is more covert and therefore harder to investigate'.

The 2017 Workplace Bullying Institute report of American statistics found that:

- 61% of Americans are aware of abusive conduct in the workplace
- 60.4 million Americans are affected by it
- 70% of perpetrators are men; 60% of targets are women
- Hispanics are the most frequently bullied race
- 61% of bullies are bosses, the majority (63%) operate alone
- 40% of bullied targets are believed to suffer adverse health effects
- 29% of targets remain silent about their experiences
- 71% of employer reactions are harmful to targets
- 60% of co-worker reactions are harmful to targets
- To stop it, 65% of targets lose their original jobs
- 77% of Americans support enacting a new law
- 46% report worsening of work relationships post-Trump

election.

The staggering costs of bullying

The obvious costs to a workplace are low morale, low productivity, high absenteeism, high accident rates, reduced engagement, management time in mediating situations, high turnover of staff and the subsequent retraining costs for replacement staff and the effect on an organisation which develops a reputation for being a bad place to work.

But the costs go further than simply HR costs.

During the transition of bringing on new and inexperienced employees, customers can be lost, quality and delivery of goods and services can be affected. If mediation fails and cases end up in employment courts, the cost of legal representation plus loss of reputation if cases end up in the press, or worse, on social media could lead to the inability to attract good people. In America they even use the term 'workplace violence' rather than 'workplace bullying'.

The costs of poor workplace practices will eventually hurt the economy.

It has been estimated that the cost of workplace bullying to the Australian economy could be around $36 billion each year when each case that hits the courts averages around $17,000–24,000 for employers.

In the UK, academics estimated the cost to the UK economy at £17.7 billion in 2007.

If we then factor in the need for ongoing help via social services when people leave organisations as a result of bullying and can no longer work, then the effect to their health becomes long term because of ongoing stress, depression, illness, insomnia, the abuse of drugs or alcohol and even suicidal tendencies.

What a lot of bullies and harassers fail to realise is that there will be a day of reckoning sooner or later. If enough complaints are laid, if turnover and absenteeism continue to be a costly problem, if the organisation starts to have challenges attracting staff because of a poor reputation, then even the most lax organisation will conclude that it is cheaper to let the bully go than to continue having the fallout from their obnoxious behaviours.

Sooner or later bullies meet their Waterloo

I watched with amazement as Kim Jong-un tried to take on Trump. Two bullies on the world stage putting on a real live gladiator show. Who would buckle first? The fact that the whole world was waiting with bated breath in case these two started a nuclear war seemed to evade them as they tried to out-tweet each other, out-threaten each other and even out-play each other.

I learned about Trump's deal making skills when I read *Trump Revealed*. The authors Michael Kranish and Marc Fisher quote numerous examples of how Trump simply does not entertain the concept of win-win; he knows what he wants and simply refuses to negotiate until he gets what he wants.

In some cases that could be laudable, but in most cases it isn't. It means he gets what he wants, but in the process he inevitably makes an enemy or ensures that the other party is left feeling humiliated. Not great for building long-term relationships at an international level.

I understand that Kim Jong-un even sent a quiet delegation to America to try to better understand Trump's modus operandi because Trump wasn't behaving the way previous presidents had done. To Trump's credit he out-blustered Kim Jong-un, which led to the talks between North Korea and South Korea and a thawing of relations between those two countries. Who knows what the outcome will be of two leaders meeting when both are used to getting their own way.

And yet it seems that for once in his life, Donald may have met someone he also doesn't understand. Donald is used to finding people's weak spots. It's his strategy.

Robert Mueller has stayed silent throughout the Russia investigation despite almost hourly tweets about the illegitimacy of the investigation. It would appear that Donald has found someone he isn't able to manipulate, bully, coerce or scare into giving him what he wants.

Mueller has run an investigation where there have been no leaks; he has amassed a team of the very best legal and accounting minds in America and they are quietly going about their work.

No matter what Trump throws at them he gets zero reaction, and I think it is quietly driving him mad. His tweets are increasing in number, emotion and ferocity each day as he tries every conspiracy theory he knows to unsettle this team.

And everything he does is failing. Failure is not in Donald's playbook.

It will be interesting to see who out-bullies Trump. Will it be Vladimir, or Michael Avanatti — lawyer to Stormy Daniels? Or will Robert Mueller simply out-play him?

> *'People who love themselves, don't hurt other people. The more we hate ourselves, the more we want others to suffer.'*
> — Dan Pearce, *Single Dad Laughing*

4

OWNING THE CULTURE AND NAMING THE GAMES

'Our scientific power has outrun our spiritual power. We have guided missiles and misguided men.'
— Martin Luther King Jr

Creating the culture of an organisation

General Montgomery ('Monty'), a senior British officer who fought in the First and Second World Wars, defined culture as 'The capacity and the will to rally men and women to a common purpose and the character which inspires confidence.'

Culture contains many components, some which appear intangible and even vaguely illusive. It really is a case of you will know a good culture when you experience it, just as you will know a bad culture when you feel it.

Culture includes the defined beliefs, values, ethics and behaviours expected of the constituents of a team or business. It reflects the attitudes and customs that have developed over time. It mirrors the 'this is the way we do things around here'.

The culture of a team, organisation or even a country absolutely starts at the top.

Understanding the power of 'values'

Leaders must know their strengths and weaknesses. They must understand that they are the mirror — that everything they do and say will be reflected in the organisation. Leaders need to be clear what they will do to be successful and what they won't do. A good leader is aware of and clearly articulates their core values so they become integral to their operation. That way, there is no ambiguity; people throughout the organisation will be crystal clear as to what to do when faced with a challenge.

Walmart famously had a rule book of how employees should behave:

Rule No. 1: The customer is always right.

Rule No. 2: If the customer is wrong, reread Rule No. 1.

In 1994 the book *Built to Last* used the following examples of successful businesses built on completely different values:

- Johnson & Johnson and Walmart made *customers* central to their ideology; Sony and Ford did not.
- HP and Marriott made concern for their *employees* central to their ideologies; Nordstrom and Disney did not.
- Ford and Disney made *products and services* their central values; IBM and Citicorp did not.

- Sony and Boeing made *risk taking* their central ideologies; HP and Nordstrom did not.
- Motorola and 3M made *innovation* their core values; P & G and American Express did not.

Johnson & Johnson apparently learned nothing from the Tylenol scandal when they were hit with yet another massive lawsuit because of harm they caused to the very people who were supposedly their core concern. They were ordered to pay US$417 million to a woman who claimed in the lawsuit that their baby talcum powder caused her ovarian cancer when she used it for feminine hygiene.

Which begs the question, how many complaints had Johnson & Johnson ignored from the woman and others like her? How many opportunities to address the problem had they ignored, delayed, denied or missed altogether? Why had they not learned from the Tylenol scandal?

Clearly somewhere along the way since the *Built to Last* book was written, their core values became lost or blurred or forgotten or buried.

The delusional games some leaders play

If you have ever worked for a boss who says one thing but does another, you will be perpetually confused and possibly even wonder if the person in question is sad, mad, dangerous or just plain delusional. It will absolutely be like walking on eggshells.

You may work for a boss or president who wants results now; they want to be made to look good, to be seen as a person who gets things done, to be a hero.

The downside of that is they are invariably engaged in rush jobs; they decry any form of preparation, they feel that strategies are for wimps and then wonder why each member of their team or administration says a different thing when asked what the goal is, or what the time frames are or even what their part in the project is. It's that famous saying: Failing to plan is planning to fail.

In Trump's administration, 'spin' has been turned into an art form. Some of the members of his team and in fact his presidency as a whole is in danger of spinning itself to a standstill with its games, lies, conspiracy theories and out and out propaganda.

We all have personality flaws; we all have 'patterns' of behaviour that probably don't serve us. Mostly though, as adults we become willing to step back from situations and to ask ourselves 'How did I set this up?' or 'What was I thinking?' or even 'Why do I keep doing this when I know it doesn't work?'

Unless we are brave enough to ask those questions, we are destined to repeat our unhelpful behaviours ad nauseam.

Eventually, after three bad marriages or five bad bosses or several bankruptcies, we may get it, that *we* could be the problem, which is when we may seek the help of a counsellor, coach or mentor, someone who will challenge us to face our patterns and become more self-aware. We may work things out when a true friend or significant other points out to us our blind spots and self-destructive behaviour. If we are smart, we listen. If we are smart, we do whatever we need to do to cease and desist from our self-defeating habits.

Changing behaviours isn't easy. I'm sure that most of us at some stage have tried to lose weight or get fitter or drink less or give up smoking and found it to be really hard. However, if what we are doing is affecting our health, our relationships and/or our career prospects, then *not* changing borders on insanity.

Every generation has a 'light-bulb' book, a book that radically changes society's thinking. For me, *Games People Play* by Dr Eric Berne was one of my own light-bulb books. I decided it was time for me to reread it to see if that would help me better understand leaders who seem hellbent on causing havoc while totally refusing to acknowledge that 'they' are possibly the problem.

The 'games' Berne refers to are better described as 'habits' – ways of interaction we've learned from our parents or behavioural habits we have adopted for whatever reason.

A positive example of a 'game' would be the late Dudley Moore, the hilariously funny comedian and part of the Peter Cook and Dudley Moore duo. Moore had physical handicaps that led to his being bullied at school, and he learned that humour kept him from the worst of the abuse. Humour was a survival game for him; it even led him into a career as a comedian. Some other 'games' are not only unhealthy but even border on being decidedly dangerous.

A few examples of 'games' from Dr Berne's book:

- Lets you and him fight. This is a behaviour where one person causes trouble between a couple of other people and then steps back to watch and enjoy the fireworks.
- I'm only trying to help you. These are the people in our lives who are determined that they know better than us how we should eat, live, speak, make decisions. These are people who, uninvited, keep telling us how to improve, earn more, be more, do more. These people are not to be confused with a significant other who lovingly points out behaviours that no longer serve us. You will absolutely know the difference.
- Let's pull a fast one on Joey. A game where two or more people gang up on a third (also called mobbing) to have a bit of 'fun'. To the people who are the perpetrators of this action, they probably see it as teasing but to the target of the game, it may be hurtful and humiliating and is an activity that could easily descend into bullying if not checked.

Children are master game players

Kids test boundaries every day. They say they don't like their parents preventing them from doing things, but at some unconscious level they know that their parents prevent them doing certain things because they care. Kids whose parents let them do anything or are so absorbed in their own lives that their children are morally abandoned are the kids who feel totally insecure. They internalise this non-intervention as being 'my parents don't care enough to keep me safe' and like the moth that keeps banging into a lighted flame, the children of non-involved parents keep taking bigger and bigger risks in the hope that 'someone' will care enough to stop them.

So is that Donald's problem, is that why he keeps creating daily dramas? Was he so starved of attention that he will do whatever it takes to keep that spotlight on him? Because to be ignored for a child is tantamount to being abandoned.

Naming the games

After working with teams for over 30 years, I know that naming the games is an incredibly courageous move for team members. At some stage of working with a team I would ask them, 'What behaviours is the team displaying that prevent you all from being awesome?' and 'What inappropriate behaviours have become normalised here?'

I often hear things like:

- People gossiping about other team members in the lunch room
- People only doing as much as they have to and never being willing to help out co-workers
- People arriving late and leaving early
- People coming to meetings late and unprepared

- People taking credit for other people's ideas.

When working with a leader, the question becomes 'What part do you think you play in this team not achieving its best results?', which is a huge question for them to take on board. It requires vulnerability, introspection, self-awareness and, more than anything, the ability to be brutally honest with themselves, to accept that they are not perfect. That they may be part of the problem but that they are also a huge part of the solution.

I heard the story of one doctor who received feedback from a peer — the feedback was that the nurses and younger doctors were terrified of him. They found him arrogant and impatient and downright rude at times, which was a shock to the person as he didn't see himself that way at all. However, once he had taken the feedback on board, he actually gave everyone around him permission to call him out. If he was behaving rationally and humanely they were to call him by his first name (let's say John), but if he was slipping into his arrogant mode, they were to call him Doctor John.

This simple process alerted him to his possibly unconscious behaviours and helped him correct them. It also made him more human to the people who worked with him and earned him massive respect for his courage to own his bad behaviours.

Naming the games and giving permission to address them requires everyone, leaders and workers alike, to look at their behaviours and to question which ones are actually productive and which ones are destructive, hurtful or damaging.

It requires us also to ask our customers and suppliers for feedback and to really take that feedback on board.

The danger of normalising bad behaviour

The problem with failing to name the games or bad habits a

team has fallen into is that the behaviours very quickly become normalised. These bad behaviours become the unsavoury side of 'that's the way we do things around here'.

When employees are supposed to start work at 8 a.m. for example, and no-one worries if they drift in as and when they feel like it, then start time becomes 8.30 and 8.45 and even 9 a.m. Employees create a new norm that no-one seems to check. Or when people in a customer service department don't rush to get back to grumpy customers because all that will mean is more complaints, then slowly but surely, no-one cares about the customer.

Bad behaviours which people have quietly drifted into over a period of time will only come to light when a new manager takes over the department, or when a particularly courageous new employee joins the team and asks awkward questions like 'Why do you do it that way?' only to be told 'That's the way we do things around here.'

So until someone calls out the bad behaviours, they will continue.

The entitlement syndrome

If you are a parent, you will be familiar with your children using the phrase 'I'm allowed'.

In the workplace, 'I'm allowed' can translate into employees rationalising arriving late and leaving early or helping themselves to stationery or any other thing that isn't tied down and that they feel is a 'right' to help themselves to.

At senior levels of an organisation this 'right' turns into abusing the company credit card or taking partners on expensive company-funded trips. Suddenly things that are classed as perks that come with the job become things that are taken for granted, and even become no longer enough to satisfy that 'entitlement' feeling. And if everyone in that organisation sees one person taking advantage of the perks, then others feel it is their 'right' also.

In Australia, a federal opposition leader in the early 1990s made a point of taking taxis everywhere rather than use the chauffeur-driven Commonwealth cars he was supposed to use; he also insisted his staff do the same.

Or consider the auto company CEOs of Ford, Chrysler and General Motors who in 2008 flew to Washington in private jets to ask for taxpayer bail-out money. One politician likened it to seeing someone show up at a soup kitchen in a limousine while wearing a tuxedo.

In New Zealand, a disgraced health board CEO was fired in 2017 after it was discovered he had spent $218,000 of taxpayer money on holidays and attending conferences around the world; this at a time when the health services were struggling to meet the health demands of his region.

And perhaps the worst example of 'I'm allowed' has been brought to light at Oxfam where several people at senior levels of the organisation were discovered not only to be using prostitutes during the tragic disasters in Chad and Haiti, but to possibly be abusing some of the young girls they were there supposedly to assist.

How does that sense of entitlement actually happen? How do people become so full of their own importance that they think ripping off a company, country or abusing children during a traumatic event is even remotely okay?

At what point does behaviour cross a line?

A huge part of my consulting would be initiated by a manager or team leader asking for help with a poor performance issue. Their concerns were usually what to say, when to say it, how to say it and what to say if the conversation started to go wrong.

In the case of poor performance of an employee, my recommendation was always to take action when:

- it directly affects the person's productivity
- it affects the productivity of other people in the team/department
- no matter how many times you have set up additional training or peer mentoring or even counselling (for home problems), performance simply hasn't improved
- it starts to affect the manager or team leader's energy and performance
- it affects company policy and procedure
- it simply becomes too offensive or annoying to ignore.

At senior levels it is more difficult than that. Who calls out management? Who dobs in their boss? Who has the courage to report a co-worker or someone above them for behaviours that bring the organisation into disrepute? Where do people go when they are pretty sure that something is horribly wrong at a management or even board level?

When people witness inappropriate action, there are several possible reactions.

They may simply turn a blind eye and get on with their own job believing it is none of their business. You could hear them say along the lines of 'It's not in my pay grade to challenge behaviours', or when challenged they may issue the famous 'I was only following orders' phrase. They may support and even encourage the action and consciously or subconsciously become enablers. They may leave.

They may become whistle-blowers.

All of these behaviours are expensive, not only to the country but to the people who are hiding behind whatever justification they are using.

People who turn a blind eye will be affected by either fear or stress; the enablers cause and encourage bad behaviours to spread; good people leaving your organisation is costly in so many ways; and whistle-blowers, although they can be intimidated and silenced for a while, will ensure the truth comes out.

So who calls out a president? Because in the case of Donald Trump, if no-one does, then the systems and processes that were put in place to ensure presidents didn't abuse their power are being slowly eroded, and dangerous precedents are being set.

> *'No-one should suffer in silence. Bullies thrive in silence.'*
> — Ricky Whittle

5

UNDERSTANDING THE ENABLERS

'Silence is not golden, silence is permission.'
— David Maxfield

The fatal attraction between people who display bad behaviours and the people who enable them

The dictionary defines an enabler as 'one who enables another to persist in self-destructive behaviour (such as substance abuse) by providing excuses or by making it possible to avoid the consequences of such behaviour'.

In any team or organisation, you will find a variety of good and bad leaders. One of the biggest problems with poor leaders is the fact that they seem to attract, or even deliberately recruit, people who will 'rescue' them or protect them and/or people who enable them to persist with their unacceptable behaviours. It's almost like there's a magnetic force between them.

I once worked as a PA to a man whose wife did their daughter's homework so she could go out and socialise with her friends. I have no idea how anyone thought that was a good idea on any level.

I've known friends who keep financially bailing out husbands/ partners/ kids. Mums who have kids in schools where only healthy food is allowed, organising takeaways for them and passing the unhealthy food over the fence at lunch time. Dads who keep loaning their car to kids who then joyride in them and leave the petrol gauge on empty.

The list is endless.

I've heard the excuses: 'Oh, they are only young once' or 'If I don't bail her out she'll go to one of those loan sharks' or 'It's okay, I can fill the car up on my way to work. He has exams coming up and I don't want him to be stressed.'

What we are teaching our kids when we do these things is how *not* to take responsibility. I know the parents love their kids; I know they want their kids to think fondly of them. The challenge is that these parents are teaching their kids to develop a 'me first' attitude. They think that it will make the kids love them more, when in fact kids with parents like this don't actually end up respecting their parents, they just see them as a soft touch.

As a counsellor I would hear wives making excuses for their husband's abusive behaviour by saying 'He doesn't mean it, he had a really tough childhood.' I'd witness partners taking on the responsibilities of a gambler by paying the bills they ran up. Partners who make sure there's a supply of alcohol in the fridge when they know their other half has a drinking problem.

I worked with one woman whose husband was seriously overweight and every time he went to the doctor he would be told his blood pressure was at dangerous levels and that he urgently needed to exercise. She would buy him gym memberships and all the expensive gym gear that he would need (a larger size each year) and he would do what he had always done — not exercise and keep eating unhealthy food. It was a case of as long as she worried, he didn't need to.

Why do people support and even encourage such obvious bad behaviour?

Enablers believe they are 'caring' for the person in question, so they constantly make excuses for them. If they misbehave in public the enabler will say they are 'stressed' or 'tired'. If they can't get out of bed because of a night of drinking, the enabler will phone in to their work saying they are 'sick' when they are actually hungover.

The worst part of being an enabler is that they tend to accept part of the blame — 'It's my fault, I know I tend to nag him/her' or 'If I didn't do [whatever the enabling behaviour is], then they wouldn't do what they are doing.'

If only enablers would take a step back and stop making excuses or taking the blame for these unacceptable behaviours, then people behaving badly would have to face the problem themselves. They would have to 'own' the problem. They would have to accept personal responsibility.

Over the past few years, we've heard of the enablers who turned a blind eye to appalling behaviours in a variety of businesses, institutions and politics.

We had the horrific case of years of sexual abuse of patients in British hospitals by Jimmy Saville. It seemed to be common knowledge that he was abusing patients (children included) and yet no-one stood up to him. And so the abuse went on for years.

We had the abuse of young female show business stars by Harvey Weinstein — another situation that everyone seemed to be fully aware of. And the most recent situation of Larry Nassar, the American doctor who abused an estimated 265 gymnasts – some who were really young children.

In 2010 the American Red Cross fundraised US$488 million for the Haiti earthquake. They promised to rebuild homes, sort out fresh water issues and set up healthcare facilities. In fact, of the 700 houses initially promised, only six houses were built. An inquiry released in 2016 discovered that 25% of the money raised was used in programme management, further fundraising and other 'expenses'.

Why don't people step in when they see inappropriate behaviour and say 'This actually isn't okay'? Why doesn't someone haul in the abusers and the mis-managers and say 'That isn't the way we treat people around here' or 'Using funds for inappropriate expenses isn't what this organisation is about'?

How long do people who see poor behaviours wait before they step in?

As I've watched countless interviews on CNN, where this station does at least try to have input from all points of view, I've watched the people who support Trump turn themselves inside out to never say anything bad about him, to never acknowledge any of his bad behaviours, to never acknowledge any facts that might upset him.

It's almost like some kind of love-blind teenager who simply doesn't want to know the bad points of their partner even though those behaviours are not only destructive, but downright dangerous.

Why did the Republican Party not realise the danger he posed? Why have they become his key enablers? When will they say 'Enough'? It is the ultimate form of denial and I have no idea if their eyes will ever open or if they will ever be willing to admit he sold them all — voters and Republicans alike — a giant bill of goods.

Jonathan Chait wrote an article for the *Daily Intelligencer* entitled 'Here's the Real Reason Everybody Thought Trump Would Lose'.

His analysis is that 'Republican insiders and donors failed to grasp the severity of the threat Trump posed to their party; many of them rallied behind obviously doomed legacy candidate Jeb Bush, or they used ineffectual messages when they did attack Trump. Or, most of all, they simply deluded themselves about the dangers he posed rather than face up to them. I never believed party insiders could fully dictate the outcome of the nomination, but I did expect them to be able to block a wildly unacceptable candidate, and they proved surprisingly inept even in the face of extreme peril to their collective self-interest.'

And to date they still seem inept or unwilling to stand up to him on much of anything.

Taking the 'pledge'

My husband was rushed to hospital while we were on a cruise around New Zealand. The norovirus struck after only a few days into the cruise, and my husband, whose health isn't the greatest, went down like the proverbial tonne of bricks.

After five days stuck in his cabin trying to shake the effects, he decided that given we had only one more day of our cruise left and that he had missed most of it, he was going to get up, get dressed and walk into 'The Mount' — a very popular part of Tauranga.

He had lost huge amounts of weight and unfortunately collapsed in one of the cafes. Fortunately, one of the tourists in the café was a doctor who rushed to his aid; an ambulance was duly called and we were whisked into Tauranga Hospital. While he was being attended to for severe dehydration, I noticed the following 'pledge' on the wall of his cubicle:

'Pledge to speak up: the care we walk past is the care we accept, so I pledge never to walk by when:

- someone is unsafe
- someone is bullied
- someone is in pain
- someone needs help
- someone's behaviour is unacceptable.

I will speak up.'

By putting these posters on the walls, Tauranga Hospital was giving every nurse, every doctor, every ambulance person, every cleaner and even every patient or visitor permission to speak up if they witnessed any behaviour from anyone that they found unacceptable. Well done, the Bay of Plenty District Health Board.

It is one thing to make a statement that a business does not tolerate 'bullying' or words to that effect, but to explain the actual behaviours so that anyone witnessing something that makes them uncomfortable then empowers them to step forward to say 'This is not okay.'

Naming the behaviours is a huge step because so many organisations wrestle with what is acceptable behaviour and what isn't. But the most vital step is to ensure the safety of the people who call out unacceptable behaviours.

Leaker or whistle-blower?

As I've followed the Trump presidency and the sheer amount of 'leaking' that seems to happen every day, even at very senior levels in this administration, it does cause me to ponder if people are actually 'leaking' information or doing the very best they can do to alert someone/anyone to their concerns.

The classic example was the 'leak' around the call Trump made to Putin to congratulate him on winning his election; a message from his closest advisers which said 'DO NOT CONGRATULATE PUTIN' in block capitals found its way into the press.

Leak or whistle-blower?

All hail the incredible courage of whistle-blowers

Clearly there are degrees of poor behaviour and unethical standards. As in the case of our arrogant doctor in Chapter 4, a word from one of his peers changed his behaviours quite easily and without the need to bring in higher authorities. He displayed some sense of awareness of his behaviours and was courageous enough to do something about them.

Taking concerns to a manager or the HR department can work really well or it can go very badly if the organisation doesn't have a policy on handling concerns, or the person listening to the complaint isn't trained in what to do next.

For example, a bully was reported to the HR person and the HR person not only took the side of the bully, they even told the bully a complaint had been laid. Or a second case where the manager decided to get the bully and the target into a room to sort things out. Needless to say the bully denied everything and the target was now in an even worse position of fear because they had dared to speak out.

Speaking out takes enormous courage as these examples show:

A doctor with an exemplary 20-year career was actually sacked by West London Mental Health NHS Trust because she raised concerns with the CEO over patient safety. After speaking out, this highly qualified doctor, a clinical lead of women's forensic directorate and consultant clinical psychologist, fell sick with anxiety and depression. She was then bullied for speaking out, lost a claim against her former employer and was hit with a £93,500.70 legal bill for costs the NHS Trust had incurred fighting her.

During his first few days on the job, a New Jersey police officer witnessed what he felt was an unlawful arrest by one of the more senior police officers and refused to testify when the case came to court. He was abused and harassed by his fellow officers, he was physically assaulted, his car was vandalised and he received threatening notes. The young police office filed a lawsuit and was awarded a US$400,000 settlement.

The senior vice president of Citigroup's Consumer Lending Group warned the board of directors of the bank about a mortgage operation that could potentially end with massive losses. Many of the mortgages were even fraudulent. He submitted weekly reports even requesting an external investigation as he became more and more concerned. Citigroup stripped him of most of his responsibilities and told him his physical presence was no longer required at the bank.

One of the most famous whistle-blowers of our generation was Karen Silkwood, a chemical technician at the Kerr-McGee nuclear plant. She became a very vocal activist in the Oil, Chemical and Atomic Workers Union so she could protest health and safety lapses which were adversely affecting the health of people in the local community. The film *Silkwood* is her story.

A recent and high profile whistle-blower is Christopher Wylie, a 28-year-old who worked for Cambridge Analytica. It would appear that Facebook gave Cambridge Analytica permission to load a 'personality profile' onto Facebook and claim the details of anyone who took the test. The problem was that Cambridge then also gained access to an estimated 50 million 'friends' of the people who took the test. It is further suggested that the company then went on to use the information they gleaned to help Donald Trump win the American election.

Wylie has appeared before a committee of British MPs to be closely questioned as to what he knew about the process and how the data was misused. Like for all whistle-blowers before him, Cambridge Analytica denied, denigrated and generally abused his reputation in the hope that he wouldn't be believed.

According to Wylie during his questioning he said that 'It is categorically untrue, that Cambridge Analytica has never used Facebook data.' He went on to say that the app they used, designed by Aleksandr Kogan, 'was the foundational data of the company. That is how the algorithms were developed. They spent a million dollars, at least, on that acquisition project.'

When reading the cases of these and many more whistle-blowers, it seems to be standard practice to fire them and besmirch their name. Many of them go through years of abuse from the organisation and/or bosses. They suffer loss of earnings and are often unable to find other work while dealing with the massive stress of taking on a large organisation. Add to that these ordinary working people can be hit with huge legal bills, which further affect their health and wellbeing. Yet all they have done is to try to do the right thing.

The tragedy of organisations committing nefarious acts is that the practices start with the full encouragement of the senior people in the organisation. They know that whistle-blowing could cost a person their job and their reputation. They rely on people *not* stepping in. And the longer the person/organisation gets away with their behaviours, the more emboldened and entrenched they become. It turns into a form of corporate and collective bullying.

The challenge is that sooner or later the truth will come out and when it does, the costs to an organisation will be massive. The tragedy is that they ignored complaints or signs or concerns in the first place. If only people could think ahead to the headline when the truth comes out. For example:

Enron Scandal: The Fall of a Wall Street Darling

Enron was one of America's largest and most successful companies. Thousands of people lost their jobs, pension funds were massively depleted and Wall Street was left reeling. It seemed unimaginable that a company of this magnitude could, virtually overnight, fall over. To this day, many wonder how a company so big and so powerful disappeared with no warning. For years Enron had managed to fool regulators and Wall Street with fake off-the-book corporations but eventually crumbled under the weight of hiding massive losses via its own fake accounting systems.

The cost of turning a blind eye

Wells Fargo was ordered to pay US$5.4 million to a whistle-blower who was fired after he reported several incidents of possible fraud by two bankers he supervised.

Amtrak was ordered to pay our US$892,000 and reinstate an employee who raised concerns about fraud by a contractor. The employee was notified that his position was being eliminated.

And some of the amounts these organisations have to pay to whistle-blowers can be eye-watering.

GlaxoSmithKline was ordered to pay a former employee US$96 million after she blew the whistle on manufacturing faults at one of their plants.

Pfizer was forced to pay out US$102 million to a group of 10 whistle-blowers when they exposed the illegal promotion of the arthritis drug Bextra.

Shouldn't these types of organisation have better standards of ethics than this, particularly health companies? Isn't it cheaper to do the right thing in the first place rather than risk these enormous payouts and the damage to their reputations?

Shame on them.

> *'Let's be clear. Educators are not walking out on your children. They are walking out* ***for*** *your children.'*
> — EdVotes.org

PART II

POLITICIANS BEHAVING BADLY

'The difference between a politician and a statesman is that a politician thinks about the next election while the statesman thinks about the next generation.'
— James Freeman Clarke

6

POWER GIVEN CAN JUST AS EASILY BE TAKEN AWAY

> *'There is a danger from all men. The only maxim of a free government ought to be to trust no man living with power to endanger the public liberty.*
> —John Adams

Did that really just happen?

I couldn't believe how many times in 2016 I said, 'I can't believe he just said that' or 'I can't believe he just did that' or 'I can't believe that just happened'.

From Trump Tower meetings with Russian agents to trying to set up back channels with Russia, to money exchanging hands in what appeared to be all manner of compromising ways. To

Trump inviting the Russians into the Oval Office the day after his inauguration, and then sharing classified information with them. The Russians must have thought all their Christmases had come at once.

I just couldn't believe that Trump or the people around him could not only think they could get away with the things they were doing and saying, but that there didn't seem to be any way to stop them in their tracks.

In 2017 we witnessed Nazi marches in America and Europe — something I'd never thought I'd ever experience. I never thought America would abandon their allies in every way possible. I couldn't believe America would leave the Paris Agreement. I couldn't believe that the leaders of two nuclear powers could insult each other via Twitter like four-year-olds. I can't believe that Trump was suggesting his campaign had been spied on, which led to his wanting an investigation, to investigate the investigation that is investigating him.

Has it only been two years? It surely felt like 10!

The Republican refrain is that the Mueller investigation has gone on long enough; Trump himself keeps up the narrative that there was no collusion, that it is just a witch-hunt. Yet so far the investigation is just over one year old. Watergate took four years to complete, the Iran-Contra deal took six and a half years; the Whitewater investigation took seven years.

Meanwhile Trump and the GOP seem to be doing everything they can to not only derail the investigation but to discredit the FBI and the DOJ, the country's established justice system, and anyone who dares to suggest that nefarious activities during the campaign are being uncovered.

Whether Trump was aware of them is still being investigated, but it does appear that if he has nothing to hide, he is putting an awful lot of time and energy into trying to block Mueller.

What no-one seems able to make him understand is that the investigation is about Russian interference, it is not about him. Surely that's a form of paranoia?

The problem with a person coming into the role of POTUS with no political background, a failure to study or care about history, a desire to change everything overnight without having any clear strategies for what replacement will look like, is that it creates a sense of power and gives him instant gratification but it creates chaos.

Politics and politicians

The dictionary defines politics as 'activities associated with the governance of a country or area, especially the debate between parties having power; activities aimed at improving someone's status or increasing power within an organization'.

It describes a politician as 'a person who is professionally involved in politics, especially as a holder of an elected office; a person who acts in a manipulative and devious way, typically to gain advancement within an organization'.

So does the dictionary description actually suggest that we can't really trust politicians? Hopefully not. At the very least there should be an expectation that our elected representatives will not do deals under the table, will not do anything to deliberately hurt the people who report to them, the people who voted for them and/or the community they reside in. Surely?

Yet every day we read about some elected official doing things that you would think even a 15-year-old would know not to do.

What happens to people who appear honest and of the highest integrity on the hustings, yet once they get into power turn into some brain-dead Neanderthal thinking they can do whatever they want, whenever they want and that there will be no comeback?

Do politicians have a responsibility to be ethical?

In my book there is no doubt. If our politicians can't be trusted, then what does that say about our society? What does that say to our children and grandchildren who are watching politicians as potential role models?

In his book *Ethics in Politics: Why it matters more than ever and how it can make a difference,* Benoît Girardin suggests that 'polls on all continents on the confidence of people in institutions show that people do not place much trust in politics and politicians. They are often seen as selfish and corrupt power-players, defending special interests instead of the common good'.

Which isn't good for voters, parties, politicians or even countries. If we regard our political representatives so poorly and they seem to be only in politics because of vanity and/or self-interest, what hope is there for society?

Dirty tactics

Where to start explaining what dirty tactics are, what they look like, what they feel like and what they sound like? How about:

Name-calling and belittling another person or race. Tweeting abuse. Spouting 'fake news' that simply confuses people and causes division. Holding on to outdated lies and perpetuating them. Attacking opponents about how they look or speak. Humiliating someone because of colour, gender or sexual orientation. Over-talking; not listening; not wanting to hear another point of view. Abusing and bullying. Harassment of any nature — whether sexual or otherwise. Abuse of power. Shaming people in front of others. Not having the backs of the people that work for you. Passing on gossip; talking behind someone's back. Blatantly ignoring someone. Refusing to help someone when to help them would be quite simple. Straight out lying. Staying silent when speaking up is the right thing to do. Using 'spin' to make bad behaviours sound better.

We've all met people like this. They drain our energy: they leave us feeling hollow and worthless.

If we are able to leave a job and remove ourselves from such a person, then we live to breathe another day, but if our families depend on the income or our career depends on us 'toughening up', then we are left feeling 'less than' and dreading every day that we have to show up and go through all the hurt and humiliation again and again, over and over.

Sadly a clear example of dirty tactics showed up in the 2017 New Zealand elections. A National (conservative) government had been in power for three terms (nine years) and the country was lauded around the world for a supposed 'rock star' economy created under this government. However, this success came at a huge cost. Investors and speculators were going crazy buying and selling the same house on the same day for massive profits. House prices rocketed, rents rocketed and many families with low incomes found themselves living in cars, not only priced out of owning a home but priced out of or unable to even afford to rent a home. Their strategy for extensive farming has caused polluted waterways that will take years to clean up.

A report from the Salvation Army found that 45% of the people who sought help from them were people who had jobs; they were not beneficiaries. What was also discovered was that some of the people seeking help not only had full-time jobs, but some of them had two part-time jobs and it still wasn't enough to cope with the ever-rising prices.

And then what became known as the 'Jacinda effect' hit New Zealand.

Four weeks before the general election, a new leader took over the Labour Party. Jacinda Ardern is just 37 years old and she absolutely refused to play any form of 'dirty tactics'. She even praised some of the outcomes achieved by the former government — unheard of from a politician. She brought a breath of fresh air to the election campaign and massive doses of 'hope' to the poorer members of our society who had been marginalised by this so-called 'rock star' economy.

The reaction from the public was immediate. It was as if someone had turned on a light in a dark room. Wherever she went she was besieged by adoring crowds. Finally, it seemed, someone actually cared about them.

However, her no-dirty-tactics strategy didn't stop the National Party from playing their own version. They bemoaned that the changes Labour planned to make to social structures would blow the fiscal budget and leave a gaping $11 billion hole in New Zealand's hard-earned surplus. They kept repeating this message on the campaign trail, instilling fear and confusion into the markets despite several economists saying the exact opposite.

Even after ANZ Bank's Chief Economist Cameron Bagrie stated categorically that there was no $11 billion gap in Ardern's proposed budget, and even after Jacinda was elected our new prime minister, the National Party doggedly played the $11 billion deficit card.

The 'win', if you like, for repeating fake facts and sowing the seeds of fear, is that a small minority of a party's dedicated voters will believe them. For a while. The 'lose' is if the new party proves them wrong and they totally lose the trust of their traditional base, then I'd suggest they are risking credibility and actually tarnishing their own brand image.

Why do it? Or is it just a sad game politicians can't stop playing because they don't know how to play the game any differently? Don't they realise how sad and bitter constantly going on about something that is clearly 'fake' makes them appear?

Shouldn't politicians and leaders alike be playing a long game? Aren't they the role models for our children and grandchildren? Shouldn't they be setting an example of debating and negotiating?

Aren't politicians supposed to be working for the voters? And if the opposition party comes up with an idea that improves the lives of a country, shouldn't they get in behind that idea to make it work? Aren't there some things that should be above petty politics?

When in danger of being caught out, deny, distract, denigrate and divert attention

Vladimir Putin seems to have become the world expert on denial.

Forty-three Russian athletes were banned by the International Olympic Committee for doping during the 2014 Olympic Games in Sochi. Grigory Rodchenkov, the former head of what became known as Russia's state-run doping scheme, blew the whistle on the process, fled to the United States and now says that he fears for his life.

Russia denied, denied, denied.

The recent poisoning of two Russians, Sergei and Yulia Skripal, in Salisbury, England, became the first time a military-grade nerve agent had ever been used on European soil since the Second World War.

Putin denied, denied, denied.

He also made the suggestion that it could have been in Britain's interest to poison the pair; allegedly £150,000 had been deposited into Yulia's bank account around the time of the poisoning hinting that perhaps she laid the poison. It strains credibility to think that this young woman would poison her father and risk a slow and painful death for £150k or any amount of money for that matter.

Putin even suggested that the UK had poisoned the Skripals. He also added that the Syrian rebels had staged the poisoning of their own families. Does he honestly believe that anyone would even remotely believe this?

The poisoning set off the mass expelling of Russian diplomats from more than 20 countries, which caused the counter-expelling of 59 diplomats from 23 countries plus the closure of the American Embassy in St Petersburg.

In the chemical poisoning of so-called 'terrorists' in Syria, among them women and children, by using the word 'terrorists' it suggests that Bashar al-Assad has a legitimate right to destroy them, but to an outsider they appear to be simply opponents of his regime.

Assad denied, denied, denied.

So just as Putin is the master of denial, Donald Trump surely is the master of crafty diversions. It appears that every time some bad news about him is about to 'break', he will find a way to take people's attention off that topic and onto another, usually via Twitter, which of course is instant. Everyone watching the first scenario now has to divert their attention to a new scenario.

Noam Chomsky hit the nail on the head when he said, 'Keep the adult public attention diverted away from the real social issues, and captivated by matters of no real importance.'

In a way, this diversionary strategy is pretty smart; it ensures the leader controls the message. The problem, of course, is that diversions will only work for a little while; sooner or later followers will get back to whatever misdeed caused the need for a diversion in the first place.

Constant diversions keep people off balance, whether that is the journalists trying to cover a particular topic or the people affected by the situation. It is another of those 'games people play' to make sure the player holds all the cards.

Leonid Bershidsky writing for the *Chicago Tribune* issued a warning that 'Trump's and his team's communications look awkward, inept, gallingly primitive. It's time to wise up: These people know what they're doing. They want their political opponents to be confused, to flail at windmills, to expend emotions on meaningless scandals to distract them from any targeted, coordinated action against specific threats. There are going to be many of these: Trump appears intent on keeping his promises. Calm concentration is needed to counteract dangerous policies.'

Alternative facts, and fake news

Kellyanne Conway, Counselor to Donald Trump, first used the phrase 'alternative facts' when asked during a press interview why Sean Spicer gave a false statement that attendance numbers at Trump's inauguration were the biggest ever, period, when there were plenty of photos to prove otherwise.

She stated that Spicer was giving 'alternative facts'. The interviewer, Chuck Todd, responded by saying that alternative facts are not facts, they are falsehoods.

Similarly, no-one had ever heard the phrase 'fake news' until Donald Trump started using it. The press have realised that if they report anything negative about him, Trump calls it fake news.

It is the duty of the press to print good news and bad. The tragedy is that something he calls 'fake news' one day, two or three days later appears to be true. How Trump thinks this plays out against his credibility is anyone's guess.

He held on to and perpetuated the Obama 'birther' movement long after everyone had proven that Obama was, in fact, born in America.

He said that 'Isis is honoring President Obama. He is the founder of Isis, and I would say the co-founder would be crooked Hillary Clinton.'

He insinuated that Senator Ted Cruz's father was part of the JFK assassination plot. When Senator Cruz learned that Trump was going to release the JFK assassination investigation papers, his hope was that the release of the files would end the ludicrous claim that his father was involved.

Does power make smart people do really dumb things?

Four university professors pondered whether overconfident people are drawn to power, or does power itself create their overconfidence? They asked a number of people in powerful positions to write detailed accounts of situations where they had power and situations where they had no power. They then posed a series of factual questions and had the subjects rate how confident they were about the accuracy of their answers.

It was no surprise that the people who naturally felt they were more powerful had more confidence and were then firmly convinced that their answers were correct. In reality, their answers were actually less accurate than people who had answered the questions and felt they had no power.

Conclusion: the subject's confidence in his or her answers was inversely correlated with accuracy.

After conducting further studies, the professors reached the disturbing conclusion that overconfident people tend to acquire roles that afford power, but the power causes them to become even more overconfident. Their recommendation for dealing with such situations was to 'humiliate the powerful'.

This seems rather extreme to me: their rationale was that the tie between power and overconfidence was eliminated when the powerful were made to feel incompetent. Oh dear, not at all the suggestion I would have expected or recommended. I'm sure psychologists and mental health professionals the world over would be equally concerned if we all resorted to ritual humiliation.

Did Theresa May move from confident to overconfident when she decided unwisely to hold a referendum over Brexit when she already had the mandate to do whatever she decided? She surely met with humiliation when the vote went to the 'leave' voters when she had felt so sure the country would want to 'stay' in the EU.

I would rather see people in power have regular peer reviews, or regular mental health checks. For sure, people in positions of great power really do need some form of checks and balances to ensure they don't move from being confident to overconfident. Organisations must set in place mechanisms which ensure people in power don't risk becoming really dumb because they have been given way too much power.

Leaders who don't listen to sage advice or study history are destined to repeat the same mistakes

Napoleon possibly didn't realise how dumb it was to try to invade Russia during winter, yet Hitler surely knew the historical result of that disastrous decision but went on to make the exact same mistake.

The decision by Japan to bomb Pearl Harbor at a stage when neither Japan nor America was involved in the Second World War ensured that both countries were now absolutely part of that war.

America brought Japan to its knees by dropping two atomic bombs on the country at a time when Japan was already defeated. It was estimated that around a quarter of a million people died on the day of the bombings, but the death toll would have been infinitely more over time as people died from the aftermath of radiation from the bombs.

Chairman Mao's idea to exterminate sparrows because he believed they ate crops, when in fact they ate the insects that destroyed crops, led to the great famine of 1958–62 and the subsequent Cultural Revolution. It was after the death of Mao Zedong in 1976 that China moved away from the one-man-for-life rule and initiated a maximum of two five-year terms for the new leader, yet China has just approved tenure for life of Xi Jinping thereby going back to the one-man-for-life rule.

Before the Vietnam War, General MacArthur said that any defence secretary who advises the president to fight a land war in Asia should 'have his head examined'. President Johnson ignored that advice and launched a jungle warfare where American troops were at a distinct disadvantage to Vietnam troops familiar with the terrain.

Robert McNamara, Secretary of Defense during the Vietnam War, said: 'Our misjudgements of friend and foe alike reflected our profound ignorance of the history, culture and politics of people in the area, their personalities and the habits of their leaders.'

That conflict was never fully resolved; North Vietnam became and remains a secretive and rogue state and the discord between

America and North Vietnam continues to this day, fifty years later.

Countless investigations came to the conclusion that Saddam Hussein did not possess weapons of mass destruction after 1991, yet in March 2003, America and Britain invaded Iraq anyway totally destabilising an already tense Middle East. Since 2003, the United States has spent in the region of US$818 billion to fund a war in Iraq that was probably unnecessary in the first place.

Which begs us to ask some questions:

- How do political parties hold their representatives to account?
- Are political parties free to vote someone 'out' if they are bringing the party into disrepute and if they are not, why not? Building trust surely is the basic foundation of leadership?
- How do we prevent people with vested interests and low ethical standards from standing for election in the first place?
- How do countries set things up so that there are checks and balances in place so leaders don't fall into dangerous behaviours?
- Is the apparent lack of ethics in politics the reason young people don't vote?
- Will a new generation of politicians fall into the same traps?

Mud sticks; how dirty tactics brought Hillary Clinton down

Over our lifetimes, I'm sure we have followed situations where it appears that someone has done something terrible only to find out later that they hadn't. They were innocent.

In New Zealand we've had a few very high-profile cases overturned once DNA evidence proved that the poor person sitting in jail for some awful crime actually was the wrong person. Imagine that. Sitting in jail, knowing you are innocent and no-one believing you.

I was devastated when Hillary lost the election. I'd never understood the vitriol around her. As the actor Hugh Laurie once said on a late show, 'I feel as though Hillary is in a play and I've missed the first act, so I don't really understand why she is the villain of the play.'

The Republican dirty tactics against her started early:

'Everybody thought Hillary Clinton was unbeatable, right? But we put together a Benghazi special committee, a select committee. What are her numbers today? Her numbers are dropping.' (Republican Majority Leader Representative Kevin McCarthy, Fox News, 29 September 2015)

What a shame the Republicans hadn't used that time to work on the Affordable Care Act they were so desperate to change so that when Trump took up office they were good to go. In the end, they had spent *no* time on the Affordable Care Act and ended up looking rather dumb and inept when they had nothing in place to fulfil their promises.

And then the Trump campaign took up the baton. They made her alleged misuse of a private server for her emails central to their message. If you read her book *What Happened*, you can follow the endless dirty tactics which even led to the phrase 'Lock her up!' even though every investigation exonerated her:

'Prior to Secretary Kerry, no Secretary of State used a state.gov email address.' (Karin Lang, the career diplomat responsible for managing the staff supporting the Secretary of State, in a June 2016 deposition)

'With respect to potential computer intrusion by hostile actors, we did not find direct evidence that Secretary Clinton's personal email domain in its various configurations since 2009 was successfully hacked.' (FBI Director James Comey, 5 July 2016)

'Our best information is that she set it up as a matter of convenience.' (FBI Director James Comey in congressional testimony, 7 July 2016)

But wait, there's more. Even though she had been berated up hill and down dale for using a non-government server, after the election it was discovered that Trump staffers continued to use unsecured devices and as I've already said, Trump himself sends out his daily tweets on an unsecured Android phone.

In Hillary's own words: 'Accusations repeated often enough have a way of sticking or at least leaving behind a residue of slime you can never wipe off. It was a dumb mistake but an even dumber scandal.'

She went on to quote the case of Ray Donovan, President Reagan's Secretary of Labour, who after being acquitted of fraud charges asked, 'Which office do I go to to get my reputation back?'

> *'Where there's a will to condemn, evidence will follow.'*
> — Chinese proverb

PART III

PRESIDENTS BEHAVING BADLY

'No man is above the law and no man is below it: nor do we ask any man's permission when we ask him to obey it.'
— Theodore Roosevelt

7

THE POWER OF PROFILING

'Sometimes I pretend to be normal, but that gets boring so I go back to being me.'
— Unknown

The truth is never about what you say, it's about what you do, and that's always about who you are

I've interviewed hundreds of people in my years as a personnel and human resources manager and sadly, in the early days of my career, made quite a lot of recruitment and even promotion mistakes.

Initially in the interview process, I took people at face value and trusted that what they were telling me was the truth. I believed every word they said when they answered my carefully prepared interview questions.

It was only much later in my interviewing career that I realised people were often telling me what they thought I wanted to hear. Maybe they were desperate for a job; perhaps they were just sick of going along to interviews that led nowhere and so were willing to say anything and agree to anything, to get whatever job I was interviewing them for.

The tragedy of employing the wrong person is that it is a lose-lose situation. It doesn't work for the organisation or business because they now have a person who doesn't fit the job because they have the wrong skills, the wrong attitude or the wrong set of values. But strangely enough, it doesn't work for the candidate either. Yes, they managed to land themselves a job, but pretty soon they are going to realise they are out of their depth skill-wise; or will feel out of sync with the organisational culture.

Whatever the rationale of people telling me what they thought I wanted to hear, I decided I had to get better at this recruiting thing. The employment contract is a bit like a marriage: easy to get into, but very time-consuming and costly to get out of.

And then I heard about a process for 'profiling' candidates, often referred to as psychometric testing.

The very first person to consider the different personality types and their behaviours was actually Hippocrates. He identified what he called the four temperaments. His aim was to better understand the health issues of each temperament and his classifications are still used by many traditional practitioners of medicine around the world.

The four temperaments he identified were:

Sanguine (relates to the blood). He found that these people are lively, optimistic personalities. They are people who love adventure and have a high tolerance of risk. They love drama and need lots of praise and high levels of attention. The downside of this temperament is that these people may struggle with overoptimism, an inability to set personal boundaries and could even be prone to addictions.

Choleric (relates to yellow bile). He noticed that these people were goal orientated, analytical and logical. Not necessarily social beings, they dislike small talk, preferring to be with people who have similar professional and intellectual interests. These people can tend to be intolerant, overpowering, poor listeners and dismissive of other people's ideas.

Melancholic (relates to black bile). These were people he noticed who liked tradition, who do not look for novelty or adventure. They are orderly, love detail and need accuracy. They also work best with clearly defined laws, rules and regulations. The downside of this temperament is that they are incredibly risk averse, need way too much information before they make a decision and wait far too long to abandon outdated systems. They become very stuck in habitual ways.

Phlegmatic (relates to phlegm). These people he realised were all about relationships. They do not like conflict and will always try to mediate so that harmony and peace are restored between family members, friends and even neighbours. Their downside is that they get sidetracked into other people's problems and tend to lose sight of their own challenges and deadlines.

Even to this day I find there is resistance to the concept of being profiled. People fear being put in a 'box' when in fact profiles don't do that. We are all a mix of the temperaments and we all have our dominant traits and our least traits. These simply translate into our strengths and weaknesses. Which we pretty much know anyway if we are honest with ourselves.

Over the years since Hippocrates first identified these four temperaments, there have been hundreds of variations on that basic profiling/psychometric testing theme. I trialled what is known as the 'bird' profiling tool when I first started working with teams. It always felt less threatening to people and even ended up being lots of fun for people who had never been exposed to such a science before:

> Melancholic = the owl
>
> Phlegmatic = the dove
>
> Choleric = the hawk
>
> Sanguine = the peacock.

You will frequently hear the term 'hawk' with regard to politicians: hawks viewed in a derogatory way are considered to be the warmongers. Trump would be classed as a peacock and Jacinda Ardern is predominantly a dove.

Profiling isn't the be all and end all; it will only ever be part of a recruitment process. References still need to be checked and it always pays to have more than one person interview a prospective candidate to offer their perceptions of a candidate.

A rule of thumb in recruiting is to beware of recruiting in our own image. We all like people like us, which is why we end up with sales teams full of peacocks and accounts departments full of owls. The problem with that is that they all think the same. Teams actually need all four personalities so that problems are solved using all the talents and viewing a problem from all angles.

For example, during a problem-solving exercise, owls are likely to ask, 'How much will this cost and what are the rules for implementation?' Doves will almost certainly ask, 'Who will this decision affect?' Peacocks could quite probably ask, 'Is there a bonus structure around this?' And the hawks will absolutely want to know, 'When will this be done?'

The beauty of using profiles in a recruitment and even promotion phase is that they show up any anomalies from what the person says at interview are their talents, and what the profile 'shows' their natural talents to be. A profile may also confirm that the person is answering questions in a way that you were thinking 'this doesn't feel right'.

If I'm looking for a salesperson (peacock) and at the interview the person assures me that they have great sales skills yet the profile of the person clearly shows that this person is actually a deeply analytical personality (owl), then sales skills are not likely to be one of their talents. I then know that the person is telling me what I want to hear.

While I was researching the topic of 'lying', I discovered the book *Trump's Brain: An FBI profile of Donald Trump: Predicting Trump's actions and presidency* by Dr Decker (a pen name), which totally caught my attention, as you can imagine.

According to the book, the FBI formed their behavioural psychology unit in 1970 with the aim of studying the minds of serial killers. They discovered that by gathering information via this programme, investigators were pretty much able to predict behaviour. As was the case even with my then lightweight profiling version, they discovered that people with a certain personality type tend to carry out fairly predictable actions from a list of pre-identified behaviours.

The FBI also identifies four personality types in their line of work. Their list is clearly a whole lot darker than any profiles I've ever worked with. They identify narcissists, predators, the emotionally unstable, and the paranoid, and over the years of amassing the behavioural data on their target subjects, they identified a scale or range of those behavioural tendencies.

The lower end of their behavioural scale is where self-centred attention-cravers lie; the middle of the spectrum is where the typical bully resides; and the more severe end of the spectrum is where criminals, murderers, cult leaders and dictators reside.

The author states that 'in honest and no uncertain terms, Donald Trump is the textbook example of a narcissist of the highest degree.' In other words, he is on the severe end of the FBI scale — which is pretty terrifying.

He suggests that all children go through a phase of narcissism, where they believe the whole world revolves around them, but that eventually they grow out of this phase. Narcissists do not outgrow the phase; a part of their brains stays undeveloped so that such people end up with the mind and body of an adult, but with the attention-craving and entitlement demands of a child. They are missing the neuro-wiring for empathy.

He uses the phrase 'paper people': every person the narcissist meets is there to serve the narcissist's needs, and the needs of the 'paper people' simply do not matter.

The very dark side of leadership

Psychology Today suggests that you are in the presence of a narcissist if that person shows five or more of the following behaviours:

- They exaggerate their own importance.
- They are preoccupied with fantasies of success, power, beauty, intelligence or ideal romance.
- They believe that they are special and can only be understood by other special people or institutions.
- They require constant attention and admiration from others.
- They have unreasonable expectations of favourable treatment.
- They take advantage of others to reach their own goals.
- They disregard the feelings of others and lack empathy.
- They are often envious of others or believe other people are envious of them.
- They show arrogant behaviours and attitudes.

Psychology Today also suggests that 50–75% of the people diagnosed with narcissistic personality disorder are male.

The problem is that because they have that initial 'charm', they can usually talk themselves into a job or a position or situation that is way beyond them; they truly believe their story and can pitch it in such a way that the interviewer (or voter) will believe it also.

The challenge for such people is that they can't sustain that charm. It will hold out until they get what they want, or thought they wanted, and just as long as things are working well. However, because they have usually talked themselves into something that is probably way beyond them, things can turn ugly very quickly. But that will never be their fault; it will always be someone else's.

So when we put global leaders such as Putin, Kim Jong-un, Bashar al-Assad, Duterte and Trump through the narcissism filter, you have to wonder not only how these people got into such positions of power, but be concerned about the terrible damage they will inflict for as long as they remain in power – which is usually way too long.

These leaders seem to combine all of the 'below the line' I talk about in Chapter 3 plus the more sinister traits identified by the FBI.

A duty to warn

The phrase 'duty to warn' is based on the name used for laws that require American mental health professionals to break confidentiality rules and report information about a patient if they believe that person may become violent and/or pose a risk to people and society.

When Donald Trump announced he was running for office, a

number of psychiatrists were so concerned about his mental health that they tried a variety of ways to alert congress to their very serious fears.

Sadly, in America there is a counter law — the Goldwater Rule — which forbids these same mental health professionals from making a diagnosis on a person they haven't been able to evaluate in person.

Dr John Gartner, a psychologist and former faculty member at Johns Hopkins University School of Medicine, said, 'The only people who aren't allowed to comment on Donald Trump's mental health are the people who are most expert and qualified to do it.' He asks, 'Does Trump need to lie to my face for me to know he lies all the time? He does lie to my face — every night. I watch TV!' Dr Gartner, a Princeton graduate and former assistant professor at the Johns Hopkins medical school, describes Trump as a 'malignant narcissist'; a condition he suggests that includes paranoia, anti-social behaviour, sadism and narcissism.

He and a group of eminent mental health professionals decided to depart from their professional organisations and the Goldwater Rule and stood up to jointly declare that they believed Trump does indeed have mental health challenges which should preclude him from ever entering the office of POTUS.

Dr Bandy X. Lee was so concerned about Trump's mental state that she called an open town hall meeting to discuss the concerns of others in the medical profession. The meeting was actually sparsely attended. Many health organisations that had agreed to attend got cold feet in the end and stayed away, probably from fear of a backlash from Trump. However, her efforts to raise concerns were supported by some powerful people.

Dr Robert Jay Lifton, a 90-year-old former Yale professor of psychiatry and author of a study about the ways Nazi doctors were perverted into killers, raised the topic of 'malignant normality', which he said were 'arrangements put forward as being normal when in fact they are dangerous and destructive'.

Dr Judith Herman, professor of psychiatry trained at Harvard and Cambridge, shared with the audience that she had written a letter to President Obama expressing alarm at the symptoms of mental instability she saw in the President-elect. She asked if there was any way to insist on a neuropsychiatric evaluation 'before this man assumes the terrifying power of a US president?'

Sadly, only two of her colleagues were willing to co-sign the letter, which went viral anyway and was read at the Women's March on Washington.

Dr James F. Gilligan, a senior clinical professor of psychiatry at NYU School of Medicine, noted that while speculative diagnoses of Trump have been made, in his words, 'one does not need a diagnosis to assess dangerousness. Anyone who doesn't flatter him extravagantly is meant to be destroyed. He engages in exploitation and violation of the rights of others, and sometimes goes as far as sadism, with no evidence of remorse.'

He observed that:

'When you add all these elements this is a class of people of whom Hitler is a member. Shouldn't we ask the question "If you knew a dangerous man was running for election, why didn't you do something?"'

8

THE TRUMP EFFECT

'Wherever I go, there I am.'
— Kermit the frog

The Trump personality: brilliant, dangerous or just plain old sad?

I've already mentioned the 'Jacinda effect' and the speed that people took her message on board here in New Zealand; and I know how I was affected by her message. It was a deep message of hope for people after what I felt were nine years of focusing only on the dollar.

The effects I felt when Trump was on his campaign trail were very different. I vacillated between anger, disbelief and incredulity, and I don't even live in America. So I wondered how Americans were feeling, what effect he was having on them.

I have to admit that his campaign message was brilliant. I believed that 'Make America Great Again' tapped into the rust belts and the no-longer-employed in a way that left others on the campaign trail breathless. His competitors on the campaign trail stood no chance. Trump is a marketer extraordinaire and an entertainer from way back. His chants of 'Lock her up!' or 'Build that wall!' had everyone in his audiences united against the establishment. 'Drain the swamp!' created a fever.

And yet anyone who knew his record and his personality must have seen past his bluster and bragging. Surely? Donald Trump showed us who he was at every stage of the presidential campaign. He was divisive, racist and misogynist; he lied, he called people names — yet people still voted for him.

We all thought he would improve on the job. He promised he would become more presidential. We felt sure he would stop name-calling, tweeting and holding grudges. He didn't do any of that.

President versus presidency

I hadn't taken a huge amount of interest in American politics until the George W. Bush years when I was totally unimpressed with his questionable invasion of Iraq. But I seriously woke up and took notice as I watched the race between Barack Obama and Hillary Clinton for the Democratic nomination. I was delighted to realise that whoever won that race was about to change history: either the first woman or the first African American would become President of the USA.

I thought finally, America is growing up. In previous years, particularly with the GOP, I seemed to see a never-ending relay race of 'Stepford' politicians: all white men, with lots of hair and beautiful teeth.

But since Trump became president I've witnessed America

wrestling with the dilemma — do we support a totally unsuitable president or do we do whatever we can to protect the dignity of the presidency?

It would certainly appear that being president hasn't changed Trump one bit; but for sure, he is changing the presidency and everything it has previously stood for, and not for the better.

I also think the GOP are turning themselves inside out not to acknowledge that they have a president who is totally destroying the 'office' of the presidency. Which is such a shame for America. Of course it would be hard to say 'This man is not suitable', but how much damage do they sit by and watch unfold? If nothing else, I hope they learn from this exercise for future campaigns so no-one like Trump ever runs again.

One suggestion: make submitting tax returns compulsory. No tax returns, no campaign trail. I think Trump would have never moved past first base. And in order for America to have true democracy, surely the Electoral College should be scrapped? Twice now they have outvoted the American voter. The American people's popular vote was wiped out when the College voted in George W. Bush versus Al Gore; and they did the same when they voted in Trump versus Clinton.

To me that's a very strange form of democracy. It's almost as if the College is patronisingly saying 'We will let the general public vote, but we know they will probably make a bad decision so we will step in and make a better choice.'

Games Trump plays

I'd literally just finished writing my book about Trump when I went on a Christmas holiday planning to put Donald aside forever; I was so over him. I wrote the book because I simply could not sit by and watch the terrible way he treats people and say nothing. And yet each day I was on holiday, I'd read or hear about yet another situation he had caused or inflamed.

He keeps doing the same things again and again. He doesn't seem to be learning and worse, he doesn't seem to even want to learn. He seems unable to work out that *he* is the cause of virtually all the dramas that keep swirling around him.

So based on the *Games People Play* book I talk about in Chapter 4, I used the games Dr Berne highlighted to see if they would shed some light on why Donald wasn't learning; why he keeps playing the same old records, why he keeps playing the same old games.

I offer the 'Joey' game as a possible example of Trump allegedly asking Anthony Scaramucci, a man who lasted barely a few days as Trump's communications director, to go on Fox News and publicly berate his Chief of Staff John Kelly; while at the same time, allegedly asking John Kelly to remove Jared Kushner, his son-in-law, and his daughter Ivanka from the White House.

He is a master at 'gaslighting', which is a way of using strategies to make a person or group question their own reality. This is a well-known tactic of domestic abusers; it is also a part of the playbook of narcissists, dictators and cult leaders.

Because it is done slowly and methodically and in such a subtle way, victims don't even realise how much they have been brainwashed. It's no surprise that the victims of domestic abuse are left with absolutely no sense of self-worth or self-esteem.

So let's examine some of Trump's games (my titles, not Dr Berne's):

- Mine is bigger than yours. The tweet where Trump boasted that his nuclear button is bigger than North Korean leader Kim Jong-un's button. Trump also suggested his IQ was higher than Steve Bannon's and that his inauguration crowd was the biggest presidential inauguration crowd ever. Period.

- I own you. His demand that the Justice Department must do as he tells them even though the Justice Department is deliberately designed to be separate and impartial from the presidency.
- I'll get you. His penchant for naming/blaming and abandoning people who report to him; people who either refuse to do his bidding or don't do whatever he wanted them to do, the way he wanted it done, even though he didn't tell them how he wanted it done in the first place; they were expected to just know.
- I win, you lose. Donald lauds himself as being the best negotiator ever, but I win, you lose isn't negotiating, it is a short-term strategy for bullying someone so that you get everything you want and the other person gets nothing. The tragedy is that if we ever need to do business with them again — or need their vote — it is highly unlikely that they will ever trust us again.
- Another fine mess I got myself into. He creates or fans the flames of the poor reporting he complains about and even over the very situations he himself creates. A classic example is the *Fire and Fury* book and the James Comey book. Instead of simply ignoring them, he tried to ban *Fire and Fury*, tweeted for days about both books, and abused both authors and all the news outlets that talked about the books. By doing this he simply gave the books air and he made both books bestsellers.
- I alone can fix this, or the God Syndrome. Throughout the campaign and according to him, no deal ever done by any other president was a good deal. In particular, any deal done by Obama came in for particular scorn. The North American Free Trade Agreement (NAFTA) between USA, Canada and Mexico was a bad deal; the Paris Agreement was a bad deal; the Trans-Pacific Partnership (TPP) between Australia, Brunei, Canada, Chile, Japan, Malaysia, Mexico, New Zealand, Peru, Singapore, Vietnam and the United States was a bad deal; and, of course, the Iran deal was a bad deal.

It would appear that Donald is actually playing multiple layers of games, for example:

- Look at me. (His way of ensuring he is always in the headlines for better or worse.)
- I will save you. (I will build a wall because Mexico keeps sending over their bad hombres, even though immigration statistics show that illegal immigration from Mexico has been in decline for quite some time.)
- You left me no choice (but to fire you, Mr Comey, because you wouldn't pledge your loyalty to me).
- If you had done xyz then I could have agreed, but you didn't so now I can't. (The battle over the Deferred Action for Childhood Arrivals, DACA, and the wall. Trump wanted US$21 billion to build the wall; the Democrats agreed to a portion of that money in exchange for giving the DACA kids a pathway to citizenship.)
- It's not fair. (The press is out to get me, the DOJ is out to get me, the FBI is out to get me, CNN is out to get me, women are out to get me, everyone is out to get me.)

And interspersed with all his other games, I notice what I'll call the 'D-day games':

> deny, distort, denigrate, destabilise, demand, destroy, damage, daunt, delay, debase, debauch, dent, decimate, decree, decry, defame, defeat, defer, defile, deflate, defraud, degrade, delete, delude, demand, demean, demolish, demoralise, deplete, depose, deprive, despise, detach, deviate, devoid, dictate, digress, diminish, disable, disband, discard, disclaim, discount, discriminate, disgrace, dismay, distort, dodge.

You get the idea. Anything but deal with what's going on; anything but tell the truth; anything but accept ownership.

Be careful what you wish for, you may just get it

There is a thought that he didn't expect to win the presidency, that he didn't even want to win the presidency, rather his thought was that by getting the massive amount of publicity being on the campaign trail would give him, he would use that publicity to grow his business. Michael Wolff, in his book *Fire and Fury*, outlines 'Trump's shock when he won; Melania Trump's tears; the chaos of the unexpected transition and the deals Mr. Trump and his associates had lined up for their post-loss plans'.

The tragedy is that because he just loves to win and can't bear losing, he played a great game. He has even said that he just loves the race to whatever prize is on the table and that once he has won whatever it is, he loses interest.

Learned behaviours

To get a better sense of Trump and his unruly behaviours, I researched his parents; after all, our parents are the ones who teach us right from wrong.

Fred, his father, was also a marketer extraordinaire. There's the famous story of how Fred rigged out a 65-foot yacht with enormous Trump signs, speakers blasting out 'The Star-Spangled Banner' and loaded with fish-shaped balloons which they threw into the water. The balloons were redeemable for US$25 up to US$250 off a new Trump home. Apparently people in the water almost rioted to get one of these very clever lures.

Today we would class Fred Trump an entrepreneur. He was a builder who had the drive to start a construction business while he was still in high school and by the late twenties was selling single-family houses in Queens for US$3,990 each. He amassed a sizeable fortune building in the Queens area and although Donald Trump likes to say that he is a self-made man, he built his own real estate business on the back of his father's reputation and his father's funding.

Donald's mother, Mary, was of Scottish heritage and in her early years of moving to the USA was a maid. With her husband's growing fortune she became a regular on the New York social circuit and was active in several philanthropic causes. He describes his mother as being one of the smartest women he has ever met. He also uses her smarts as the reason he has had problems with women because no woman he has ever met has been as smart as his mother — according to him! Trump also credits his love of 'showmanship' to his mother. She too had a love of big, flamboyant hair.

Both his parents were hardworking and thrifty immigrants; they both came from poor stock and worked their way up the financial ladder. Which makes it all the more surprising that Trump has such disdain for immigrants.

The only parenting information I could find was a suggestion that Fred Trump was arrested at a KKK (Ku Klux Klan) rally though was later dismissed from all charges, a suggestion that his mother was often not around, and an article where his mother asked, 'What kind of son have I created?' when he was going through a very messy and public divorce from his first wife, Ivana.

In the same article a friend recalled how Donald's father was always around to watch him play while a friend of Donald's older brother Fred Jr remembered how the kids 'rarely saw their mother but did see a lot of the housekeeper'. Is this perhaps the cause of his lack of respect for women?

It was clear that Fred was Donald's hero. In one interview with Donald Trump, when asked what his father would have thought of his run for president, Trump replied, 'He absolutely would have allowed me to have done it.' This from a man in his seventies.

Although proud of what his father had achieved in Queens, Donald had his sights firmly placed on becoming part of the Manhattan high society scene. In his *Art of the Deal* he writes about the numerous attempts he made to become a member of Le Club; eventually he became a member but the rich high society of New York did not accept him. They found him to be brash and gaudy.

Did this rejection from the smart set release his need to pay people back for slights and hurts? I wonder if his flashy, braggadocious ways were the very things that put his name in lights, but were also the very things that turned Manhattan off him?

And New York seriously gave him feedback as to how much they shunned him when he won 9.7% of the vote in Manhattan and Hillary Clinton won 86.36%.

We are the sum total of everything we believe about ourselves

When I watch Donald I see a 72-year-old child testing boundaries to see how far he can go. Even when people give him what he says he wants, he then changes his mind and says 'That isn't enough.' So is he really saying 'I'm not enough'? Is it possible that Donald has an internal emptiness that nothing will ever fill, that nothing will ever be 'enough'? Is that why he craves so much? Not even becoming POTUS seems to have filled the void.

The sadness of Donald when all his strange behaviours are acted out every day is that he so desperately wants to be 'liked' and yet does everything he can to ensure he isn't. Could his declaration that the whole world was laughing at America really be that he feels the whole world laughs at him?

Are all these behaviours simply a desperate cry for someone to 'Please hurry up and stop me before I self-destruct'?

So will/can leaders like Trump, leaders who behave badly, ever change? Will they ever listen to a true friend, a significant other, a coach or a mentor? In Donald's case, I fear not. In the first year of his presidency he hasn't seemed to grasp that the presidency isn't a reality TV show where you have to check the daily ratings and have a cliffhanger event so people will tune in to the next episode. It isn't reality TV where audiences tune in to watch dramas — this is real life and he is charged with looking after all people, not just the rich and the corporates and his family.

The ripple effects of his presidency

In schools it is suggested that many of the gains by anti-bullying initiatives have been lost since he came into power. The Human Rights Campaign (HRC) presented alarming results of its national post-election survey of the effects of Trump's bully behaviour. They cited an increase in youth bullying during and since the 2016 campaign.

After surveying a diverse group of 50,000 youths aged 13 through to 18, they found that 70% of respondents had witnessed bullying, which included hate messages or harassment, throughout the campaign period and in the immediate aftermath of Trump's election victory.

Among those who witnessed the bullying, '79 percent said it occurred more frequently following the start of the campaign.' The bullying effects of the Trump presidency — dubbed the 'Trump effect' — can be devastating. He takes regular aim at minority groups, people who are not in a position to defend themselves.

It appears that the parodying of Trump's name-calling and threats of deportation have caused some of the bullied children to suffer panic attacks. Children under stress do not learn well; the long-term effects, particularly as the deportation of some of their parents started taking place, will be detrimental for years to come, if not generations to come.

In the health sector, prior to his coming into power, 93% of the non-elderly population were covered by Obamacare or the Affordable Care Act (ACA). Notwithstanding his campaign promise to scrap the ACA and his inability to do so despite holding the senate and the house, his administration is slowly chipping away at all manner of health benefits for the elderly, as well as middle- and lower-income families.

Doctors' surgeries have seen a rise in patients' stress levels. David Williams, a Harvard expert on social influences on health, told an NBC News interviewer that studies have shown stress levels have risen since Trump's election. Not just with his opponents, but with supporters also. He suggested that 'events came together to create an unprecedented moment with the levels of hostility being reported'. Quoting a variety of recent studies he suggested that stress levels shot up right after Trump's inauguration in January. Twenty-six percent of those presenting with stress symptoms were Republicans and 72% were Democrats, but more minorities than whites. Two-thirds of all American adults said they were stressed when they thought about the future of the US.

And one of the more extreme effects of Trump making things up is that others emulated him. Conspiracy theories took off.

A story circulated that Hillary Clinton was running a child sex slave outfit from a pizza shop. This led to Edgar Maddison Welch from Salisbury, North Carolina, storming a DC pizzeria where Clinton's presidential campaign chairman, John Podesta, occasionally dined. Welch walked into the Comet Ping Pong armed with an AR-15 and a handgun and opened fire at the floor and walls. Once the police arrived, he told them he wanted to investigate a paedophile ring and to 'rescue the child sex slaves'. He apparently surrendered peacefully when he realised they didn't exist and that a Democratic presidential candidate was not abusing children in the basement.

My Gran used to say, when I was four years old and fighting with my best friend, Margaret, also four years old, 'This will only end in tears.' And I fear this is exactly what will happen for Donald as he fans the flames of fake news and altered reality and lays the groundwork for his never-ending conspiracy theories and increasing paranoia.

Why he lies and the damage that causes

I've been stunned and amazed at the sheer number of lies he tells on a daily, even hourly, basis.

He tells lies which can easily be shown to be lies — like his absolute conviction that millions of people voted illegally even though it has been proven that this is not the case. Or that he was wire-tapped by then President Obama — he wasn't. Or that the FBI had implanted a spy into his campaign; they hadn't.

But because he is Trump he believes that if he says something often enough, people will believe him. And tragically, it appears he is right.

He now denies he fired James Comey because of the 'Russia thing' yet he was interviewed live, on television, by Lester Holt of NBC News for all the world to see. He said, 'I said to myself you know, this Russian thing with Trump and Russia is a made-up story, it's an excuse for the Democrats having lost the election.'

And now he is denying it.

I'm also puzzled by the way he tends to talk about himself in the third person at times, almost as if one part of him distances himself from another part. It does seem strange, but that's way above my knowledge to analyse; it just seems odd.

I wanted to better understand why people lie — not just Trump, but others that I've met over the years. We all tell the occasional porky. It may be that we've been invited to something we don't want to attend so we say that we have a prior engagement when we actually don't. Or we may not want to upset a friend when she asks if an outfit suits her and so we say it does when we probably think the opposite.

Leaders may lie to push through an agenda: 'The merger with xyz companies will not cause any job losses' and then the pink slips start being handed out. Managers lie to keep hold of their workers saying 'We can't afford any pay rises this year but I can promise you that next year we will be in a position to increase wages' and then the manager gets a raise and a new company car because he has kept wage rises to a minimum. Politicians promise all manner of things when they are on the campaign trail and once in office develop selective memory.

Do we class these actions as lies or broken promises? Spin doctors are masters of prettying up lies: 'This is not a demotion, it is a way for you to move to a different department and learn new skills.' Yeah, right.

I checked out numerous articles on Google and found that there appears to be a lying continuum from the little white lies we all tell, as in 'I would have loved to come to your party but I'm already booked to go somewhere else', down to lies which could send a person to jail or cause a war.

It seems that we lie because:

- we want to be polite and/or we don't want to hurt someone's feelings
- we don't want to have to do something so we offer an excuse

- we want to impress or inflate our importance. This happens on most CVs where the most common lies are about the power we had and the salary we earned
- we want to cover up something — like a purchase we couldn't afford, an affair we had or even a criminal record.

Even in all of these scenarios, I'd have to think there would be limits as to how far we would go with a lie. Surely for most of us, our conscience would be activated at some stage and we would either admit to the lie or at the very least stop perpetuating the lie?

So then I researched information on a deeper and more sinister level of lying. We lie:

- when we want to gain power over someone or something
- when we want to manipulate or cheat someone for personal gain
- when we choose to blame someone for something we did and then sit back while they take the fall
- when we want to hurt someone or get back at them for something, by spreading falsehoods about them which could affect their jobs, lives or prospects.

The problem when someone in a leadership role lies is that what they say can have a profound effect on their followers. For example, in 2015 a study led by Briony Swire-Thompson at the University of Western Australia presented 2000 adult Americans with one of two statements:

- Vaccines cause autism.
- Donald Trump says that vaccines cause autism.

It was discovered that the participants who were Trump supporters showed a stronger belief in the second statement. When these participants were given data from a large-scale study which proved that vaccines do *not* cause autism, they were asked to re-evaluate their belief in that statement. Initially they accepted that the statement was false, yet when tested again a week later, the Trump supporters had gone back to their original belief, that Donald Trump says that vaccines cause autism so it must be true.

Leaders really do have a duty to check facts and tell the truth because the ultimate problem with lying is that every lie chips away at a person's reputation or credibility. After lying the first time, they then have to tell more lies and more lies to cover up the first lie.

If someone lies to us, we may believe them the first time, but once we realise that we've been lied to, the next time that person makes a statement about anything, we are not going to be quite so trusting. And if we discover that this person has actually lied to us several times, even when they tell us the truth about something we won't believe them. A classic boy-who-cried-wolf scenario.

There's a lovely saying: 'Fool me once, shame on you; fool me twice, shame on me.'

Finally, and sadly, according to research there are habitual, compulsive and even pathological liars; people who have made lying their way of life and where they just keep adding bigger lies to the original lie even in situations where telling the truth would be just as easy.

In an article by David J. Ley, PhD, he suggests that pathological lying isn't actually a clinical diagnosis, but lying to such an extent that it actually doesn't even serve the person, can be a symptom of a personality disorder.

All the more reason, then, to ensure that a person who appears to be a habitual liar does *not* become the President of the USA.

Past behaviours usually predict future behaviours

None of us is perfect. We all have personality flaws, we all make mistakes, we all have 'patterns' of behaviour that probably don't serve us. Mostly though, as adults, we become willing to step back from situations and ask ourselves 'How did I set this up?' or 'What was I thinking?' or even 'Why do I keep doing this when I know it doesn't work?' Unless we are brave enough to ask those questions, we are destined to repeat our destructive behaviours ad nauseam.

As we learn to understand our own patterns of behaviour and how they serve us or not, most of us learn to set personal boundaries; we have lines we know not to cross or paths we have learned not to take. No matter how stubborn we are, we have to take responsibility at some stage of our lives. Blaming others won't work forever.

In Trump's case, shouldn't four, five or even six bankruptcies have woken him up to the fact that perhaps he really isn't a great businessman?

The *Washington Post* investigated his bankruptcies and discovered that his Taj Mahal casino, which opened in April 1990, defaulted on interest payments just six months later and ultimately filed for bankruptcy in July 1991. Two Atlantic City casinos were declared bankrupt in 1992 and his Plaza Hotel in New York also declared bankruptcy in 1992. Trump Hotels and Casinos filed for bankruptcy again in 2004 at which stage Donald Trump had accrued US$1.8 billion in debt and finally Trump Entertainment Resorts declared bankruptcy in 2009.

So on my counting that amounts to nine bankruptcies, though I understand Trump counted the first three bankruptcies as just he one. Shouldn't that number of bankruptcies have taught him not to over-extend, or not to set up way too many deals at the one time?

He was well known for overpaying for properties and assets; if he wanted something, he bought it no matter the price. In *Trump Revealed*, we also find out that he owned limousines, a yacht, five helicopters and a private plane — all on borrowed money. At the same time he was launching golf courses, hotels, casinos, a Trump airline and fitting them all out with luxurious items — all on borrowed money.

He knew nothing about airlines when he bought 21 planes, but that didn't worry him one little bit. In 1990 he owned 22 assets but only three of them were making any money. At this stage his net worth was minus US$295 million.

But none of this seemed to trouble him or even slow him down.

Apparently, according to the authors, he had loans out with over 70 banks and was in debt to the tune of US$3.2 billion; his net worth was minus US$293 million.

None of the banks was aware of the other banks until the day they realised the extent of his debt. Sadly they also realised that he had set the deals up often without collateral, so that if one loan fell over, all the loans would fall over. The banks involved would have lost millions of dollars.

So is that clever negotiating, smart selling, greed or insanity?

We've already said that changing behaviours isn't easy. I'm sure that most of us at some stage have tried to lose weight or get fitter, or drink less or give up smoking, and found it really hard. However, if what we are doing is affecting our health, our relationships and/or our career prospects, then *not* changing really is insanity.

Why could voters not see through him?

As I watched Trump on the campaign I kept thinking, surely

people will start walking out of these massive auditoriums as he berated, belittled, humiliated, etc. But they didn't. Even now two years down the track of his winning the election, it would appear that the same number of people form his base, the same percentage of people follow him, the same group of adoring fans can find absolutely nothing wrong with anything he does or anything he says.

I've watched countless interviews on countless channels to see if I could sense a shift in these Trump devotees; to see if they were finally realising who he was and what he was. I kept looking at the faces of people who swore black was white, that he is their hero and that the press and the Democrats are just out to get him.

The *American Sociological Review* conducted a study which showed that 'even when voters believe a candidate is untruthful, they can still view that candidate as an "authentic champion of constituency".' (Oliver Hahl, Minjae Kim, Ezra W. Zuckerman Sivan, "The Authentic Appeal of the Lying Demagogue: Proclaiming the Deeper Truth about Political Illegitimacy," *American Sociological Review,* January 10, 2018. doi.org:10.1177/0003122417749632)

The researchers surveyed 400 people: 177 of the people were acknowledged Clinton voters, 186 Trump voters and 39 people who voted for others — the aim was to study why Trump supporters view him as authentic. The final conclusions were that the people who voted for him justified his lies as forms of 'symbolic protest', and the more they viewed him as an act of protest, the more they believed in his authenticity.

As in the previous test regarding vaccinations, people were asked to view a tweet from Trump which said that 'the concept of global warming was created by and for the Chinese in order to make U.S. manufacturing non-competitive'.

Among his supporters, 61.8% found his statement as highly

authentic and only 5.9% viewed the statement as highly inauthentic. A significant number of his supporters also agreed that he did not literally mean the statement in his tweet, rather they felt it was Trump's way of challenging the elite establishment.

Of the Clinton supporters, 95.5% found the statement highly inauthentic.

Ultimately I felt that his voters fell into one of two categories: the white men and women who were perhaps not as well educated and had been disenfranchised by their loss of jobs; and the supremely rich who felt that Trump was the man who would make sure their wealth was if not improved, then absolutely left intact, wealthy Republicans who also appear to be predominantly white yet who decry any form of help for poorer families. Two groups at polar opposites surely. You would think that it was impossible for both groups to see him as their saviour.

And so whether we call this out as a racial issue, the 'white' thing does seem to be a theme within his party and his voters. His followers, whether rich or poor, do seem to be people who like the prospect of a white status quo or, as I heard someone define it, the rise of cultural grievance.

The eight key areas where Trump is literally carving out the heart and soul of America

1. His hatred of the free press

From day one of his presidency, Trump has called out the press. 'Fake news' has become his catchphrase; a phrase no-one had heard of until Trump went on the campaign trail. A phrase that was named 2017's Word of the Year.

Almost daily, as the press discover something about him from a variety of sources, he calls whatever it is 'fake news' only for the world to discover days or even hours later that in fact the breaking news is 'fact'.

A free press is at the heart of democracy. It's no mistake that dictators ensure that the press is silenced. The leaders of Turkey, North Korea, Russia and China are known for at best throwing journalists in jail to at worst, silencing them through violence and even assassination. Trump has made veiled threats about 'jailing' journalists and in a tweet suggested that he may take away their credentials — in other words they wouldn't be allowed to attend press briefings at the White House.

It would suggest that his administration is going down a slippery slope when CNN and AP (Associated Press) were banned from an EPA meeting with Scott Pruitt; the excuse being that there weren't enough seats, yet the press gallery area was apparently half empty. The reason Pruitt didn't want them there could have had something to do with the topic of the meeting — water pollution. Given Pruitt's record of denying there is a climate problem and his cosying up to the fossil fuel sector, it would seem that the meeting wasn't to prevent water pollution, rather to allow it.

2. His bizarre recruitment and replacement strategies

When a government changes in America it appears that all the overseas ambassadors can be recalled so the incoming administration can put their own people in these key roles around the world. Traditionally the incoming president would leave existing people in place until such times as they found replacements. Trump fired every single ambassador the moment he took oath. Which seems to be such a massive loss of expertise. It was often at dinner parties and embassy cocktail parties that multi-billion-dollar deals would be discussed or where intelligence would be picked up. You would think these positions would be non-partisan given the incredibly important role they play.

If it's true that he was not expecting to win the presidency, then it is no surprise that he was ill-prepared to find the 591 replacements required to fill these key roles. By removing all these vital people in what seemed to be a fit of 'Obama pique', he left serious economic and national security gaps and risks for America.

As Trump has made his various appointments, it is bizarre to see that he seems to choose the person who is not only least qualified for the particular role, but is also, it appears, totally anti the very department they have been selected to oversee.

Donald has famously said that he hires great people and then chooses not to trust them. That could be translated into 'I set people up for failure because that way I will always look better than anyone I hire'.

It is also interesting to see that many of the people he would like to hire are choosing to say 'No thanks'. They know only too well that their reputations will be on the line if they choose to work for a man who takes on people and then refuses to listen to them; a man who ridicules his staff publicly and then within weeks ditches them via Twitter.

He fired his Secretary of State, Rex Tillerson, this way. How humiliating; how unprofessional.

Scott Pruitt is not a scientist; he is a lawyer and climate change denier. He was given the role of heading up the EPA. According to the *New York Times,* Pruitt has said that 'he alone will decide what is and what isn't acceptable for the agency to use when developing policies that affect health and the environment'. And according to his Wikipedia profile during his campaign for Oklahoma Attorney General, he received major corporate and employee campaign contributions from the fossil fuel industry.

Trump appointed Teresa Manning to oversee the Planned Parenthood department. Manning is an anti-abortion and anticontraception activist. She was charged with overseeing the 'Title X' programme, which provides family planning funding for four million poorer families or those without health insurance. Apparently she resigned in January, which must be great news for families.

According to reports in the *Daily Intelligencer,* he put Lynne Patton, who organised his golf tournaments and planned his son Eric's wedding, in charge of the Department of Housing and Urban Development's New York and New Jersey office. He put Keith Schiller, his personal bodyguard, in charge of Oval Office operations. He nominated his personal pilot, John Dunkin, to lead the Federal Aviation Administration.

He put his son-in-law Jared Kushner in charge of all manner of key departments, including negotiating peace in the Middle East. And he offered the job of running the VA (Veterans Affairs) department to his personal physician; the man who conducted Trump's first physical exam as President. Admittedly Ronny Jackson is a Rear Admiral with an impeccable services record; he was physician to Obama and Bush before he took over looking after Trump, but is he even remotely qualified to run a department with 365,000 staff and a US$200 billion budget?

Eventually Ronny Jackson withdrew his application for the position and he was subsequently removed as White House physician.

3. The loss of scientific expertise

In David Cay Johnston's book *It's Even Worse Than You Think,* the author outlines the terrifying ways Trump is stripping America of its scientific people and knowledge. In his very first budget, scientists around the world were horrified when Trump cut off one fifth of the National Institute of Health budget; a massive US$6 billion reduction. He cut billions of dollars of spending from basic research and biomedicine at a time when China, India and other nations are doing the exact opposite. According to Johnston, 'the opening of one coal mine or even a hundred cannot come close to matching the economic benefits that can flow from a single research project'.

4. The cost of his homophobia and xenophobia

Trump is doing everything he can to rid the armed forces of transgender Americans, citing the medical costs they create. It is estimated that there are approximately 2500 active transgender troops with a further 1500 in the reserves. Costs of covering their healthcare are estimated to be around US$8.4 million, which in the scheme of the annual military budget someone described as a 'rounding' number. When the announcement was made, Secretary of Defense Jim Mattis quietly told these troops to 'hold the line'.

Fortunately, on 30 October 2017, Judge Kollar-Kotelly deemed Trump's transgender ban to be a violation of their 5th Amendment rights and she duly granted a preliminary injunction to keep the policy from going into effect while the court case moves forward.

It is estimated that there are around 11 million undocumented immigrants in America.

According to Ben Gitis, the director of Labor Market Policy at the American Action Forum, to physically deport this number of people would cost between US$400 billion and US$600 billion. But it would seem that the flow-on costs to the American economy would create economic ruin for many sectors.

The National Milk Producers Federation warned that around half of the people who work on dairy farms are immigrants. The cost of losing this number of workers would add a further US$32 billion to the bill, and this in turn could double the cost of milk, hitting consumers directly in their pocket.

What I've found unbelievable is people who have been hardworking contributors to their communities being ejected simply for not having the paperwork, not for having committed crimes; some of whom even had successful businesses and employed staff. People who have married and had American children being sent to a country they have no connections with leaving their families with no provider.

But that has paled into nothingness now we see women and their children being separated at the border; children going to one part of the country, their mothers being kept in jail not knowing where their children are or even whether they are safe. There could be nothing more heartless than this.

5. His effects on workers and workplace safety

Trump's promise on the election trail was to look after 'the forgotten man'. He campaigned on jobs, and voters believed him. If ever there was a better example of don't listen to what people say, always look at what they do, then Trump's determination to get rid of as many safety regulations in as short a space of time as possible reflected this truth. From day one in office, he started his 'war on regulations'.

The OSHA (Occupational Safety and Health Administration) website had traditionally posted all deaths from workplace accidents to make sure that accidents and fatalities are not seen as just statistics in a dull report but real-life, human situations. David Cay Johnston, in *It's Even Worse Than You Think,* states that Trump's Labor Department quietly closed down that webpage, a decision that so incensed Jordan Barab, who had been Obama's number two man at OSHA, that he, as a private citizen, took it upon himself to keep track of workplace fatalities and exactly how people had died. He called the site 'OSHA won't tell you who died in the workplace. We will'.

And so began a process to delay, repeal or weaken any

regulations that in Trump's view 'killed jobs' but in reality, killed or maimed people. His rationale? That regulations slow down economic growth.

Yet according to the IMF in its World Economic Outlook, removing workplace regulations that keep people and the environment safe would slow economic growth rather than speed it up. They rationalised that the outlook for US growth was less rosy because of 'difficult-to-predict US regulatory and fiscal policies and geopolitical risks'.

6. His need to be at 'war' with everyone

I've often wondered how many fights one person can want on their hands at any one time. I can't even begin to imagine the stress factors of his daily rants on Twitter, his seemingly weekly firings, the number of lawsuits he must be facing from all manner of people for all manner of reasons.

By 5 May 2017, just four months into his presidency, the *Boston Globe* had counted 134 lawsuits filed in Federal Court since his inauguration. Women are suing him in record numbers. Three high-profile lawsuits hit the news in early 2018; Karen McDougal, Stormy Daniels and Summer Zervos are all standing up to him. Meanwhile the Mueller investigation chugs along despite every attempt to derail it by the Republican Party and Trump himself.

As I write this, Trump is at war with Jeff Bezos, founder of Amazon and CEO of the *Washington Post*. It would appear that on the surface Trump is anti what he sees as Amazon taking advantage of the US postal service by negotiating a deal for special rates (isn't Donald the person who wrote *The Art of the Deal*?) and their failure to pay taxes. Though it seems that his real beef is more to do with point number one in this chapter – his hatred of the free press, because Jeff Bezos also owns the

Washington Post, a newspaper that regularly calls out Trump for all manner of poor behaviours.

Should it be the right of a president to single out a company?

Apparently Amazon shares lost billions during the tweet tirade. In an interview with Larry Summers, the former President of Harvard, Fareed Zakaria asked for Summers' thoughts on this particular vendetta. Was Trump right to call out what Trump suggests is the abuse of power of a big company, or was this outside what he should be doing? Summers' reply was 'It's not the job of the president to go on a jihad against a company because he doesn't like a newspaper owned by the CEO.' He went on to say that he found this situation 'the most distressing and long-running trend of the Trump administration and its shift in approach from the rule of law to the rule of the deal'.

The challenge for someone like Trump who had run his own business and where his word was law, where no-one ever dared to stand up to him or disagree with him, is that he has now entered a world where he is pitting his wits against some of the toughest and smartest leaders in the world.

So in the middle of dozens of other controversies, it seemed to be out of the blue that he decided to start a trade war with China. Trump announced 25% tariffs would be put on 1300 Chinese imports: toys, electronics, shoes, clothing and furniture. Which set off another tit-for-tat exercise when China threatened to put tariffs on cars, aeroplanes and soybeans — the top agricultural export from America to China.

The subtle and smart move made by Xi Jinping is that he will be putting his tariffs on all the products that come from territories that voted for Trump in the presidential election. So a double whammy for Trump.

And the effect of all the trade war threats that are now being hurled backwards and forwards ensures that the stock market is adversely affected daily. So if we think people don't cope well with confusion and inconsistency, then the markets abhor it. It was James Carville, one of Bill Clinton's campaign strategists, who famously said, 'It's the economy, stupid.' So if Trump thinks that he can mess around and play his power games in this arena, he may be in for his biggest wake-up call ever.

7. His willingness to throw people under a bus at the slightest provocation

He threw Jeff Sessions, his Attorney General, under the bus because he (quite rightly) recused himself from the Russia investigation. He threw James Comey under a bus because he wouldn't swear loyalty to him. He threw Steve Bannon under a bus because Bannon was featured on the cover of the *Time* magazine and was said to be the brains of the Trump campaign. He threw Scaramucci under a bus within days of employing him because he did way too many TV interviews and Trump felt he got way above his station. He threw Reince Preibus under a bus because he was too short and didn't look the part of his chief of staff. His current chief of staff, John Kelly, keeps being threatened with the bus but seems to have managed to avoid it so far.

But all his staff are at risk of the bus, because Trump simply doesn't have any coherent policies on any aspect of his presidency. This leaves key members of his staff in all manner of awkward and embarrassing situations as they try to explain policies that have never been explained to them; or which are changed on a whim. And woe betide any staff member who ever apologises or suggests that the administration made a mistake.

Larry Kudlow, presumably with Trump's permission, suggested that Nikki Haley had suffered 'momentary confusion' when she presented the Trump administration's approach to Russian sanctions to the UN Assembly. Haley, however, is one person who fearlessly stands up to Trump, his administration and his inner team. Her response? 'I don't get confused.' Kudlow apologised — Trump did not.

Day after day we witness the lack of clear communication strategies, stories that get changed by the hour, explanations that are different depending on who is asked and how long it is since they got the last change of mind from Trump. Poor Sarah Huckabee Sanders is sent out every day to do the press briefing where it is totally obvious she has to spout a party line that can leave her looking foolish at best, a liar at worst. They don't seem to have heard the expression 'singing from the same hymn sheet'.

8. His desperate need to undo everything President Obama put in place

For me this has been the strangest yet most telling of his strange behaviours. His vendetta against Obama started, it seems, with the birther movement. He was determined to prove that Obama had not been born in the USA and so should never have been made president. He held on to this belief long after it had been proven beyond any doubt, that Obama had been born in Hawaii — one of the states of America.

Was his hatred of Obama because he was probably one of the most popular presidents in recent history? Was it because he was a Democrat? Or was it because Obama was black?

Is his 'Make America Great Again' slogan really a covert plan to make America white again?

It wasn't difficult to work out during his campaign rallies that he was a misogynist; his derogatory comments about women are legendary. It also became clear that he was also a racist when, on his first day in office, he brought a huge chunk of the world to a standstill with his 'Muslim ban'.

Since the end of the Second World War, it has been unthinkable for the majority of society to show any Nazi tendencies in public. There are followers, of course, but for the most part they have lived out their fantasies behind closed doors. Until Charlottesville. On 12 August 2017, the leader of the free world stood back as people freely marched with Nazi banners and slogans; and when a young woman was run down in Charlottesville by a white supremacist, he said there were good people on both sides.

His immigration levels have been slashed to the bone yet he is still demanding his wall. Surely, even he must realise that trying to rid America of everyone of colour simply is never going to happen; it is surely too late to do that. The world is now a mix of numerous cultures and all the better for it, in my view.

A meeting was held in the Oval Office during the early stages of Trump's presidency. It was to thank three chiefs representing the 400–500 Native Americans from various tribes who had served in the US Marine Corps during the Second World War as 'code talkers'. By transmitting messages over radio or military telephone in the Navajo language, they were able to pass messages which the enemy were not able to transcribe. These Native American tribes had been virtually wiped out by the early settlers, yet despite that history, they risked their lives during the war.

This was the very first time anyone had acknowledged their contribution, and Trump used their special historical moment to denigrate Senator Elizabeth Warren by calling her Pocahontas. It was a joke that went horribly wrong. It was insensitive, rude and embarrassing on so many levels, not only to these three elderly men who were there to represent their various tribes, but also to use the opportunity to denigrate a female senator.

Has he amassed a following or has he actually created a cult?

He famously said that he could shoot someone on Fifth Avenue and people would still support him, so whether that was a throwaway remark or a touch of genius in knowing his base, it surely said that he knew he was on safe ground no matter what he did or what he said.

Wikipedia explains what happens when a cult is forming or has formed:

'A cult of personality arises when a country's regime — or, more rarely, an individual politician — uses the techniques of mass media, propaganda, the big lie, spectacle, the arts, patriotism, and government-organized demonstrations and rallies to create an idealized, heroic, and worshipful image of a leader, often through unquestioning flattery and praise. A cult of personality is similar to apotheosis [divinisation], except that it is established by modern social engineering techniques, usually by the state or the party in one-party states. It is often seen in totalitarian or authoritarian countries.'

If the Republican Party doesn't wake up to what he is doing, and very few of them show any signs that they are willing to challenge him, then they are being just as complicit in unleashing this cult as his base.

Is he making America irrelevant on the global stage?

The problem with his nationalist desires is that he has created a vacuum in world leadership that China or even Russia will gladly fill in a heartbeat.

His threat to pull out the soldiers currently fighting in Syria with barely a week's notice would have created mayhem. He must be aware of what happened in Iraq when then President Bush pulled troops out too early; that decision gave birth to Isis and a terrorist movement like nothing the world has ever seen before.

In a way I can understand that, when he considers the cost of having American troops in various theatres around the world either as peacekeepers or as soldiers on the ground. He must look at the vast savings that could be made by bringing everyone home. The US war in Iraq cost US$1.7 trillion and with an additional US$490 billion in benefits owed to war veterans, expenses that could grow to more than US$6 trillion over the next four decades counting interest.

War costs. Trump is strangely cost conscious, particularly given his previous bankruptcies or rather because of those bankruptcies. But certain decisions have to factor in the benefits as well as the costs. America to a degree set itself up as the world's policeman, and for that the democratic world is truly grateful, but that role comes with responsibilities and benefits. Some of those benefits are that American troops can be stationed in sensitive areas as a deterrent to rogue countries i.e. the troops in South Korea closed positioned to let North Korea know that they are being watched. To suddenly abandon all the areas in which America has a presence will have all manner of long term costs. And if he is trying to save America money by bringing troops home, why then is he increasing the military budget? He plans to ask for US$716 billion for defence in his 2019 budget.

He seems to want to pull out of every trade deal ever made — why? Because he didn't negotiate the deals? Because he thinks he can make better deals?

From everything I've read about his deal-making skills, I'd suggest he doesn't actually negotiate deals; deal-making requires an attitude of win-win. Trump makes up his mind what he wants, and that's it — if he doesn't get what he wants, he walks away. He is 100% I win, you lose. He seems to have no hesitation in bullying, manipulating or otherwise humiliating the other person.

The upside of this strategy is that he gets what he wants, the downside is that he alienates the person on the other side of the deal and, I would assume, leaves long-lasting mistrust and even resentment. And then what happens when he needs that person again?

He proved what a terrible negotiator he is when he called the Mexican President to demand that Mexico build his beloved wall and was not impressed when the Mexican President point blank refused. He keeps being told by all around him that America doesn't need a wall, that it won't work and that it is a waste of taxpayer money, but it has become one of his fixations.

We were able to watch him negotiating live on TV over the DACA children. He said, 'Bring me something that will work and I will sign it.' A bipartisan group did just that. First he vacillated, then he changed his mind, and now he is refusing to sign anything at all. So almost two million kids are now being used as a political football.

Surely his decision to pull out of the Iran nuclear deal is illegal?

If you enter into a contract and then decide you didn't get a good deal, surely that's a case of tough luck? A deal was negotiated and it appears that Iran has kept to its side of the bargain, but Trump decided it was a bad deal and removed the USA from it. All other signatories — UK, France, China, Russia, Germany and the EU — have said do not pull out, what we have isn't perfect, but it is working. Those pleas fell on deaf ears.

The Iran deal was a perfectly legal contract; it wasn't perfect, but it was a legal document. Will the other signatories honour that contract and ignore America's decision to walk away just as the CPTPP countries did over TPP?

Because now North Korea or any other country that might be looking at negotiating a deal with America has just seen how America treats signed contracts. Why would they sign? Why would they trust anything this president says knowing that he could change his mind again, on a whim, and just because he can, or that future presidents who decide that Trump didn't negotiate a good deal can also decide to pull out?

The loose lips strategy of this administration seemed to be the final nail in the coffin of any potential summit with North Korea when John Bolton suggested that Trump might be looking at using the Gaddafi model of denuclearisation; a model which pretty much saw the demise of Gaddafi and his regime.

Is Trump himself being 'played'?

It was clear that the Russian intervention in that 2016 election was designed to undermine Western democracy, because I'm pretty sure the last thing Putin would want to risk is the Russian populace demanding legitimate elections which could see him being voted out of office.

It has become clear that Putin's intention was to divide America; cause chaos, have the political parties savaging each other. That is exactly what is happening; Putin must be very happy.

Putin's bigger hope though was to have Trump become President rather than Hillary Clinton because she had promised to make his life a misery via more sanctions. It must have seemed fairly obvious to even to the most unsophisticated follower of politics that Putin desperately wanted Trump as President in the hope that he would lift the existing sanctions Obama had imposed.

So although Putin didn't get the sanctions lifted, Trump very quietly delayed imposing the new sanctions congress imposed for the Russian interference, making the rather weak statement that 'the threat of sanctions was already acting as a deterrent'.

Really?

I think Putin well and truly won that round.

Trump simply refuses to acknowledge interference, presumably because he thinks by acknowledging interference, his presidency is illegitimate. It isn't. Trump was elected fairly and squarely by the Electoral College. By ignoring the interference, by trying to railroad the investigation by doing everything he can to discredit his own judiciary, making them the bad guys, he is virtually giving permission to the Russians to interfere with any and all future elections.

At this moment in time, the summit between Trump and Kim Jong-un is on and then it is off. Trump desperately wants the publicity of this summit to keep his base assured that he is still the tough leader they voted for. He has even had coins printed to mark the signing of a peace treaty. A bit premature, surely. Kim Jong-un has already won round one of this battle by getting the sitting president of the USA to come to a meeting with him. No previous president would ever give him that legitimacy.

But if Trump uses his age-old deal-making strategies, it seems safe to predict that he will do no planning or preparation, he will involve no diplomats or experts on North Korea; he will rock up, make his demands, leave no opening for any negotiations and walk out.

That's the Donald playbook.

The problem with that is Kim Jong-un wins — he will get his legitimacy from Trump showing up and Trump will have to walk away empty-handed.

Will he be remembered as a leader, a would-be dictator or a martyr?

The definition of a dictator is: one holding complete autocratic control; a person with unlimited governmental power; one ruling in an absolute and often oppressive way.

On that basis I think it is Trump's dream to be a dictator. Just imagine the power he would have. As I watched the first year of his presidency I kept recalling memories of being the mother of two- and three-year-olds, and my later dismay at trying to manage teenage tantrums. That's what Trump's behaviours reminded me of.

When two-year-olds and teenagers play their version of 'I'm allowed' or 'I want it and I want it now' games and don't get what they want, they either throw a tantrum or take the it's-not-fair stance, which is classic martyrdom.

If Donald wants something, he expects it; he demands it, no matter what the cost or the consequences. If he doesn't get it he sulks, he admonishes, he blames and he tweets. Think of that military parade — he attended the parade in France with President Macron and had a lovely day, and so he decided he wanted one of those. Fortunately wiser heads have been working in the background to discourage the idea and the parade may go the way of the 'wall'.

I've said many times that I think Hillary Clinton had a very lucky escape when she lost the election. Imagine the sulking and the backlash and the tantrums he would have thrown if she had won. He still berates her on a regular basis and she lost the election.

I kept watching his attraction to the various tough men around the world, like Duterte, Putin, Erdogan, and it was clear he so wanted to be one of them; to be able to demand whatever he wanted and it would be given to him, no questions asked. My fear is that unless Republicans finally find the courage to say no to him, if the Mueller investigation is destroyed in some way, if no-one ever calls him out, then he will win. America will have their first dictator.

However, if his dictator aspirations fail — and I pray they do — then rest assured the world will see his very own full frontal martyr game.

Being a martyr allows you to avoid guilt and shame. It says you can let go of the need to take personal responsibility. It allows you to choose not to grow. It says you can point your finger at whoever or whatever you like to blame for your finances, your health, your inability to hold down a job or to be a success.

So at some stage, when we hear Donald say 'They wouldn't let me; I tried everything I knew; I did everything I could to look after you, my people; but in the end the injustice of our system just beat me down. Poor me', you will know that is the last card in his pack.

And tragically, his base will buy it.

> *'The difference between a democracy and a dictatorship is that in a democracy you vote first and take orders later, in a dictatorship you don't have to waste your time voting.'*
> — Charles Bukowski

PART IV

LEADERS AND POLITICIANS BEHAVING NAIVELY

'Rank does not confer privilege or give power. It imposes responsibility.'
— Peter Drucker

9

OUR FUTURE REALLY IS COMING, READY OR NOT

'A person often meets his destiny on the road he took to avoid it.'
—Jean de La Fontaine

Facebook made to face facts

Back to the power of personality or behavioural profiling.

In 2014 Aleksandr Kogan, a university lecturer, developed an online personality quiz. He persuaded Facebook to promote the quiz and Kogan was then able to harvest the information and data from around 40 million Facebook users. The actual numbers have varied depending on which news outlets you follow, but the *Guardian* ventured to suggest that the number of people affected could be as high as 87 million users.

Kogan then, without Facebook permission, joined forces with UK company Strategic Communications Labs (SCL) and its US subsidiary Cambridge Analytica (CA), a company funded by Republican financier Robert Mercer.

Together these companies were able to analyse the treasure trove of data Kogan had captured and use it to influence voters. As a side note, Cambridge Analytica were also involved in helping the presidential campaigns of Ted Cruz and Ben Carson.

As more and more of this information started to become public, the *Intercept* published an article saying 'Facebook failed to protect 30 million users from having their data harvested by Trump campaign affiliate'.

Because I didn't know the background as this story broke, my first reaction was that Mark Zuckerberg must have been incredibly naive to think he could give or sell access to private and personal data to an outside company and that they could be trusted not to abuse the information.

Zuckerberg is a young man: Facebook was his first job. All credit to him for creating a multi-billion-dollar business that revolutionised how we all communicate.

The challenge with anything new, particularly a new technology product or service that takes off like a bush fire, is that not enough thought is given to or even an awareness of the pitfalls that may lie ahead. In such a scenario, leaders and managers of such companies really are making decisions on the run. They literally have no previous terms of reference and no-one to ask 'How did you deal with xyz?'

Once the story truly hit the headlines, Zuckerberg was summoned to face a two-day congressional hearing on what had gone wrong.

I watched a tech-savvy young man being questioned by older

senators who knew little or nothing about technology and had probably never used Facebook in their lives. They were demanding answers but hadn't a single clue as to what questions to ask. Even worse, it seemed they hadn't bothered to involve any younger people who did understand Facebook, to discover what questions they should ask.

A case of the naive meeting the clueless.

And so, because our politicians don't know enough about technology and the potential dangers of it being abused, we watched social media being subverted by a number of entities with vested interests, including, it would seem, Russia.

Some have called what happened in the various elections around the world in 2017 nothing short of cyber war: an attack on a country's election process and even on democracy itself. *USA Today* alleged that Russia meddled in the affairs of 27 European and North American elections since 2004. These attacks ranged from disinformation campaigns to all-out cyber attacks.

These entities were savvy about technology. The data they were able to gain via all manner of tactics was ultimately used to target and send precise messages out to individuals with the sole purpose of swaying their thought processes and ultimately affecting the way they chose to vote. In fact the information was so finely targeted that a husband and wife sitting on the same settee could be sent different promotional information via their smartphone as a result of their Facebook information and activity.

These companies didn't even need to be devious in some cases; they were able to gather enough information just from people's 'likes' to be able to predict the race of a person with around 95% accuracy and their political party with around 85% accuracy . A *Washington Post* article reported that 'it took only 90 bored social media consultants in St. Petersburg to help sway voters toward Donald Trump in the 2016 election'.

Facebook was eventually shamed into re-evaluating their advertising policies as a result of this possible Russian interference in the US election. Though Facebook initially denied knowledge of what was happening, it was discovered that the ads were actually paid for in roubles so it should have been fairly obvious who was placing them.

Turning a blind eye to the clear warnings

It appears that Zuckerberg and his COO, Sheryl Sandberg, had been warned in October 2016 by Zuckerberg's long-time friend and mentor, Roger McNamee, that they faced enormous risks if they allowed personal information to be harvested. Zuckerberg's response was that 'we're not responsible for what third parties do' to which McNamee replied that if the 1.7 billion followers they had at that stage decided that giving their data away was a bad idea, then Facebook would be absolutely responsible.

They chose to ignore the advice and people started closing their accounts once the Cambridge Analytica story broke. Apple co-founder Steve Wozniak immediately closed his Facebook account, incensed by what he saw as the misuse of people's data. In an interview with *USA Today* he said that 'Users provide every detail of their life to Facebook and Facebook makes a lot of money off this. The profits are all based on user info but the user gets none of the profits back.'

I'd always wondered why Facebook, as a business model, didn't just charge every user US$10 per annum to use the site — with two billion users that would have earned US$20 billion per year. They wouldn't have needed advertisers and they wouldn't have risked not only their reputation but the security of their customers' data and possibly even democracy itself.

Failure to ask 'What if?'

The problem with business owners and managers being so busy and stressed is that they rarely take the time to ask 'What if?' Start-up technology companies have usually raised millions from investors and shareholders and will be aware that time is money.

Decisions need to be made in the moment in any business; every business has targets to meet for the next quarter; owners and managers know that they are in the spotlight, results are required. So thinking through the potential 'what ifs' probably isn't seen as a priority. They simply fix things on the run.

And so decisions are made with hopefully the best intention but rarely with any thought or even awareness of what could happen a year or so down the track.

With a technology start-up, four questions need to be asked:

- What have we actually created here?
- How will it be used?
- How could it be abused?
- What steps do we need to put in place to ensure we don't lose control of our creation?

Imagine if Zuckerberg and his team had asked 'What if Cambridge Analytica misuses our customer data? What if they onsell it?' What are our risks? How will our customers feel if their data is abused? How do we make sure the data isn't abused? Why are we selling our data in the first place?'

I'm sure if they had asked any of those questions, they would never have allowed this company to access sensitive customer information. And because they didn't ask, they are now facing the massive backlash of two billion people whose information has been put at serious risk.

Note: At the time of writing on 23 April 2018, 40% of

respondents admitted they have or will abandon Facebook, while the same proportion said they will continue to use the platform. The remaining 20% were undecided.

Learning on the run

I think that the biggest challenge for any leader, whether a leader of a business or country, is the sheer speed of technology and the corresponding ability for all of us to be vulnerable to bad news updates via social media on a daily basis. One false move, one unhappy customer and within seconds, an unhappy customer can reach thousands if not millions. One mistake hitting the news could ensure that most leaders are just one tweet away from disaster, which must be a terrifying way to live and work.

But I come back to base camp for me, which is that if leaders have good solid values and a clear strategic goal, then decision-making won't be difficult. The problem is if they don't have such self-imposed and self-aware boundaries and they literally make decisions based on pure emotion or raw greed, then crisis is inevitable.

Truth will rise to the surface (eventually)

Back to leaders behaving naively.

Does Trump honestly believe, even with all his diversionary tactics, that he is above the law and won't be found out in all the various cover-ups he seems to have instigated and the daily conspiracy theory he touts? He may be keeping his base happy but more and more people in his party are either resigning, being replaced by Democrats or finding it more and more difficult to defend his actions.

Do the Republican senators who are still enabling him honestly think that their voters won't eventually have had enough and vote them out?

Does Putin honestly believe that he can interfere in the democratic elections of other countries and even to resort to poisoning people on foreign soil without any form of retribution?

Does Kim Jong-un honestly think he can keep launching rockets at will while claiming it is America that is being provocative? Do both Trump and Kim Jong-un honestly think their childish tweets and insults won't have consequences; at best global outrage, at worst nuclear war?

Does Bashar al-Assad honestly think that in the end he won't pay the price for the endless slaughter of his own people?

Not even despots reign forever; eventually they all meet their destiny. Sooner or later poor business leaders are removed; sooner or later poor country leaders are voted out, usurped, ousted or jailed.

> *'Enter, stranger, but take heed*
> *Of what awaits the sin of greed,*
> *For those who take, but do not earn,*
> *Must pay most dearly in their turn.'*
>
> — J.K. Rowling, *Harry Potter and the Sorcerer's Stone*

10

IF NOT ME, THEN WHO?

> *'When you see something that isn't right, not fair, not just, you have to speak up. You have to say something, you have to do something.'*
> — John Lewis

Do we get the leaders we deserve?

Just because some leaders want to go backwards or hold on to the status quo for as long as possible, so others will drag us all into the future, probably kicking and screaming, but doing what a leader should be doing — taking us forward, making us face reality, as it is not how we would wish it to be.

It was Malcolm X who asked, 'If not me, then who? If not now, then when?' And so if you look around your community, your country and even around the world, and you are not happy with the leadership you see, what can you do about that?

I've been pretty harsh on Trump in my previous book and I make absolutely no apologies for that. I think he is an appalling leader and I'll continue to voice that opinion until such times as he either improves (which is highly unlikely given his personality) or resigns or is replaced or removed from office.

If we've taken on a job where our manager turns out to be a monster, we can leave and find another job. It isn't so easy when we are faced with a country leader who seems hellbent on finding a daily war to fight, either within his own party or with allies or even with other countries. But we can still fight back. We can tweet, or email our local politician; we can go onto social media and demand better behaviours, and at the appropriate time we can get out and vote.

Why aren't young people voting?

Perhaps they got the vote too easily. They haven't had to fight and struggle and march to get the vote. They don't live in dictatorships and yet the challenges of today are their challenges. They are going to be left to deal with the various messes several generations of leaders before them have created, so why are they not shouting from the rooftops that current politics and policies are the very things that are destroying their planet and their future?

I can see that voting once every three years probably doesn't seem to count for much. And I can see that they think their one little vote can't make much of a difference. But it can. If no-one bothered to turn out to cast their vote, then the same government would stay in power ad nauseam. Even if all our vote does is to say 'I'm not happy with the current government', then hopefully enough people will create a change of government.

I've even wondered if taking the vote off the under 25s might make them fight to get it reinstated and then actually value it and use it?

I can also see that listening to politicians sharing their policies isn't exactly riveting, but it *is* important to know what they stand for.

In Hillary Clinton's book *What Happened,* she heard from the mother of one young woman who didn't bother to vote because she didn't think Hillary was very 'entertaining'. No wonder Donald won. He was a reality TV star, an entertainer — he has the habit of saying 'Tune in, folks, for the next nail-biting episode and find out what havoc I'm about to cause!'

Have we really brought up this generation to believe that life is about being 'entertained'?

And yet I know that once awoken, this generation can mobilise within hours and create miracles.

Sam Johnson, a 22-year-old student at the University of Canterbury, mobilised 9000 student volunteers within hours of the massive Christchurch earthquake via social media. He went on to win the 2012 Young New Zealander of the Year Award for his efforts.

The online social media world is their world and somehow we have to encourage that energy and motivation into electoral voting and making a difference to political outcomes (which they probably find boring) and politicians (who they probably find equally boring). Imagine what they could do to change the world.

The good news is that a lot more young people are entering politics:

- France: Emmanuel Macron, 39
- San Marino: Matteo Fiorini, 39
- Estonia: Jüri Ratas, 39
- Ireland: Leo Varadkar, 38
- Bhutan: Jigme Khesar Namgyel Wangchuck, 37
- New Zealand: Jacinda Ardern, 37.

Some points of interest about these new leaders: Jacinda Ardern is the first woman in New Zealand to be a Prime Minister while expecting her first baby. Leo Varadkar is the first leader of Ireland of Indian heritage; he is openly gay and has just led Ireland to bring about abortion reform in a traditionally Catholic country. We also have the youngest politician ever elected here in New Zealand: Chlöe Swarbrick is just 23 years old.

Hopefully these young and diverse leaders will encourage other young people to step forward and get involved. They are the future.

Huge advances have been made in the 2017 UK elections. A record number of female MPs won seats and for the first time ever, the number of females in politics in the UK has surpassed males.

Understanding followership

No-one totally rules the world, even though some people like to think they do. We all follow someone or something. We expect an awful lot from our leaders but do we ever consider what type of 'followers' we are? Do we realise that as followers we have responsibilities also?

Definition: Followership is 'the ability to take direction well, to get in line behind a program, to be part of a team and to deliver on what is expected of you. It gets a bit of a bad rap! How well the followers follow is probably just as important to enterprise success as how well the leaders lead' (John S. McCallum).

I've noticed particularly when a country leader is elected, how quickly their allure appears to wear off and voters turn against them. President Macron of France is a perfect example. He rode into power of a wave of patriotic enthusiasm and within a very short space of time found his popularity waning.

Emmanuel Macron when first elected was the darling of France. He was young, handsome, fresh. And yet within a very short space of time, the voters turned on him.

According to the Ipsos Game Changers poll for the French daily *Le Point*, of those surveyed, more than half of French people questioned disapprove of the French President's performance: 54% were 'dissatisfied' with the 39-year-old's actions less than six months after his landslide victory against far-right leader Marine Le Pen; 58% of voters questioned in the Ipsos poll said France was 'neither better nor worse off' since Mr Macron was sworn in as President in May.

Why do we turn against our leaders so rapidly? Are we followers too impatient or do we just have unrealistic expectations of what is possible and how long things take? Don't we as followers have a responsibility to trust the people we have elected? Shouldn't we at least give them breathing space to settle into the role? Or is it that once we've voted for something we then wish we hadn't and so we attack the person or system rather than take personal responsibility and wonder why we voted for them in the first place?

Brexit is a living, breathing example of overnight voter remorse. Apparently the very day after the leave/stay referendum, more than one million people regretted their vote and wanted to change their minds. This was a prime example of checking the facts and thinking things through before we cast our vote because once you have voted, that's it. No going back.

Do we as followers have to do a bit of 'growing up'?

Do we really understand the power of our vote?

It took enormous pain and sacrifice for women to get the right to vote in the late 1800s and early 1900s.New Zealand was the first country in the world to give women the vote. Yet 100 years later, countries like Saudi Arabia, the Vatican, Brunei and the United Arab Emirates still forbid women to vote or stand for election.

In fact, in true dictatorships like North Korea and Zimbabwe, no-one has the right to vote; not men or women.

Voter turn-out in Western democracies is reducing dramatically and we have to wonder why that is. Australia, Argentina and Belgium have made it compulsory to vote. And this observation from Wikipedia could possibly persuade other countries to do the same:

'In Australia, voting prior to 1924 accounted for between 47% and 78% turnout of eligible voters; following the introduction of compulsory federal voting in 1924, this figure jumped to between 91% and 96%.'

The responsibilities of followers

- We need to thoroughly research the leader we are voting for; their past behaviours, reputation and credibility.
- In the case of American voters, to not just follow one source of information, i.e. Fox News versus CNN, but to explore all of the reputable sources before we make a decision, and then having made our decision based on good research to stick with it and give the person a chance. We must absolutely beware of all sources of fake news and avoid listening to conspiracy theorists: they will seriously mess with our heads.
- As voters, we are adults, not children. So we need to stop looking for someone to be our mother or father or hero, or our guardian.
- We need to be willing to hear the harsh truths. Trump promised to bring jobs back — a great thought. As an example he promised to reopen coal mines. This, for coal miners who had been put onto the scrapheap as mines closed, must have been joy to their ears. But coal is becoming more and more obsolete as newer and cleaner technologies take

over. Did the coal miners really think he could do this? Did they take responsibility after the closures of the mines to look for work in other sectors, to take responsibility for their own upskilling and retraining? Sadly, as humans we don't like to hear the truth — and yet surely, that is the very thing our leaders should be arming us with?

- And the personal responsibility people must accept if they choose not to vote — if you haven't bothered to vote, then you can't complain about the outcome!

George Stephanopoulos, ABC News chief anchor, interviewed James Comey just before his book *A Higher Loyalty* was due for release, and Comey was asked if he thought Donald Trump should be impeached. His reply:

> *'I hope not because impeaching and removing Donald Trump would let the American people off the hook. People in the country need to stand up and go to the voting booth and vote their values.'*

So to followers everywhere, please use your vote; remember, people died for you to have that luxury.

Some people are standing up to him

I keep wondering why the Democratic Party are not standing up to him more forcefully; or if the American system simply doesn't facilitate their opposition parties to have much of a voice. If so, that is a real tragedy because just as every country needs a vigilant press, it also needs a vigilant and empowered opposition. That's the only way power is checked and underhand activities are brought to light.

Each day I'm staggered that there seems to be no way to hold Trump to account; to stop him doing the things he does, saying the things that he says and doing deals in all manner of unsavoury ways.

If the Republican Party won't hold him to account, surely the Democratic Party must?

The CEO of Merck, Kenneth Frazier, one of the few African American CEOs of a Fortune 500 company, resigned from the American Manufacturing Council to protest Trump's silence over Charlottesville. For him he said it was a matter of personal conscience to take a stand against intolerance and extremism.

John Feeley was the US Ambassador to Panama when Trump came into office. Feeley was a career diplomat, a former Marine Corps helicopter pilot and a man of principle.

He recalls that when they first met, Trump asked him what Panama was doing for America and once he realised that it was such a small country and probably wasn't going to be of any vital importance to him or America, he moved on to talk about Trump hotels. This is an extract of Feeley's resignation letter:

> *'As a junior foreign service officer, I signed an oath to serve faithfully the President and his administration in an apolitical fashion, even when I might not agree with certain policies. My instructors made clear that if I believed I could not do that, I would be honour bound to resign. That time has come.'*

11

LEADERS BEHAVING CONSCIOUSLY

'At any particular time, leaders are operating from either fear or love.'
— Jim Dethmer, *The 15 commitments of conscious leadership: A new paradigm for sustainable success*

Are you a conscious leader?

What exactly is a conscious leader?

Understanding this kind of leadership takes us right back to Chapter 1 where I talked about knowing yourself inside and out, warts and all, strengths and weaknesses, biases and prejudices, and any other aspects of yourself that are relevant to your being a whole person, a sorted person, a person who is comfortable in their own skin.

A conscious leader will have resolved all childhood baggage, faced their demons, got rid of habits of self-sabotage and ego trips, dissolved their fears of failure and/or success and will literally walk to their own drumbeat.

I've always loved this quote from Iyanla Vanzant:

> 'You've got to know your "thing" and you've got to call it a "thing" whether it is meanness, nastiness, unforgiveness, arrogance, ego, resistance, rebelliousness or defiance. Everybody's got a "thing" and once you call it your "thing", you can give it a place or dismiss it.'

This fits with my 'naming the games' concept. Once you have given something a name and called it out, it really does lose its power over you.

When I think of conscious leaders, the late John McCain and Michelle Obama come to mind. Both have taken their fair share of flak from this president and his followers but both have held their heads high, risen above the tragedy that is name-calling and belittling, and they have both truly retained their dignity.

John McCain was a navy fighter pilot during the Vietnam War. He was shot down, badly injured, captured and endured five and a half years in what was affectionately known as 'The Hanoi Hilton'. He was tortured on a regular basis. When the Vietnamese discovered that his father was a high-ranking officer in the US Navy, they used that knowledge as a form of propaganda to offer him early release, but McCain refused to leave; he chose to stay until all his men were released alongside him.

McCain was awarded the Silver Star, Bronze Star, Purple Heart and Distinguished Flying Cross. As a politician in the House and the Senate, he was known for questioning and challenging anything he felt needed to be challenged. Not just from a party point of view, but from a personal values point of view. He called for the withdrawal of troops from Lebanon and didn't hold back his criticism of the administration's handling of the Iran-Contra deal.

He openly criticised Donald Rumsfeld, then Secretary of Defense, declaring that he had no confidence in the man. He was also the man responsible for increasing the number of troops in Iraq by 20,000, which his supporters believe increased security there.

He was the man who famously brought down Trump's repeal of the Obama Care Act with the words: 'I take no pleasure in announcing my opposition. Far from it. The bill's authors are my dear friends, and I think the world of them. I know they are acting consistently with their beliefs and sense of what is best for the country. So am I.'

Michelle Obama is a lawyer and writer. As the wife of the first African American president, she took her fair share of racist flak but always rose above any insults that came her way. She supported her husband with grace and dignity, is an amazing speaker and has the ability to call out this president and his administration without ever naming them. She chose to support Hillary Clinton during that incredibly divisive campaign against Donald Trump and became known for the use of her phrase 'When they take the low road, we take the high road'.

I could imagine if she ever ran for President in her own right, she would be a shoo-in, but then why would she want the job? Why would she want to take the racial abuse and personal slights? She is way smarter than that. I just hope, and am sure, she will make her mark in other ways.

The paradox of being a good leader in one area and a poor leader in another

This is not an uncommon situation. The belief is that if a person can be successful in one area, they must surely have the skills to be successful in another area.

Not always.

Particularly in politics it seems that the leaders people want during times of war are not necessarily the leaders they want in times of peace.

David Lloyd George, a Conservative Prime Minister, has been credited with winning the First World War against Germany, but afterwards was seen as a man who had not only broken promises but had also failed to deal with mass unemployment and industrial unrest that hit the UK after the war.

British society changed massively after the First World War. Many people wanted things to go back to how they had been before the war, but the people who had left their jobs as farm labourers or people in service had seen a new world open up before them; they didn't want to go back to how things had been. The class system had fallen apart and there was an undercurrent of desire for social change that the Conservative Party failed to notice. To their detriment.

Knowing when your time has come

Winston Churchill was absolutely a man for his time. Any British citizen who knows anything about the Second World War will be familiar with Churchill's 'We shall fight on the beaches' speech, or his 'Never give in. Never, never, never.' He took Britain into a war that the majority of his political party didn't want; but he persuaded them with his famous 'This was their finest hour' speech.

When British soldiers were being annihilated by the German army at Dunkirk, it was his idea to mobilise every small boat in the south of England to rescue them. What a sight that must have been to those weary soldiers.

He kept people motivated through the mass bombings of London, and Liverpool and any other port that was being raided nightly, via his regular broadcasts on radio.

He was the politician who first brought about a minimum wage system. He was an accomplished artist and writer. He was awarded the Nobel Prize for literature and was named Greatest Briton of All Time in a poll conducted by the BBC. Yet this was a man who suffered from depression. What he called his 'black dog'.

And yet he also qualifies for my next leadership category …

Knowing when your time has gone

What a pity that Churchill didn't step down as soon as the war was over. Because just as the end of the First World War created massive social change, so post-Second World War people wanted a total change in their lives also. Winston and the Conservative Party missed that shift — again. Just as Lloyd George had been seen as a leader for war but not a leader for peace, then Churchill was viewed in the same vein.

According to Dr Paul Addison, an Honorary Fellow (history) at the University of Edinburgh:

> 'Labour's landslide victory in the 1945 general election remains one of the greatest shocks in British political history' acording to Dr Addison an historian at the University of Edinburgh. He attributed this loss to the fact that 'studying and understanding 'war' was one of Churchill's greatest passions and that military victory was by far the most important of his goals

> 'And to Britain's eternal gratitude, he achieved victory against all the odds when Hitler and the Germans were defeated. However, when the war was over and business-as-usual resumed, Churchill appeared to be left without a clear vision for a post-war Britain. So the rest is history. Labour swept into power; his day was over and the Labour party's time had come.'

The message of the Labour Party was 'Let's face the future', which appealed to the masses far more than the Conservative slogan of 'Finish the job', whatever that was supposed to mean.

Understanding life after the spotlight and the art of giving back

I remember once watching an interview with a Miss World winner the month after she handed her crown over to someone else. She was distressed because her phone had stopped ringing; invitations to events and gatherings had dried up and she was terrified about what the future held for her.

As we've just seen, both David Lloyd George and Winston Churchill were a bit like fashion designers — one day they were in and the next day they were out.

What do people who have been at the peak of their mountain do once their day is over? I guess some will fall into depression; others will hopefully take time out to think about their what next; some may have been smart enough to have their what next already planned.

After the Watergate scandal and his enforced resignation, Richard Nixon faced health and financial problems, but went on to write and sell his memoirs; he carried out paid speaking engagements and returned to the world stage.

Jimmy Carter served only one term in office but went on to work for humanitarian causes, wrote books, and in 2002 was awarded the Nobel Peace Prize. Even now at age 92 he is still involved in charitable works and building homes for disadvantaged people.

And we've just heard that the Obamas, instead of doing what presidents have traditionally done by opening a library, decided to open a centre for citizenship in Chicago. Their aim is to encourage ideas from young leaders, involving them in thinking about what they want going forward and, hopefully, what they are prepared to do to achieve those goals.

My point in reflecting on post-leadership is to remind anyone who is currently in a leadership role that there is life after the spotlight, but also to remind them that nothing lasts forever. In particular, I'd like to remind them that the reputation they build during their tenure can make the difference between having a successful what next and a miserable one.

The aim of leadership surely is to leave a legacy; to have it make a difference that you lived at all.

When you see an opportunity to make a difference, take it

I had felt sorry for Jeff Bezos when Donald Trump was taking him on via Twitter. He wasn't being derided for his business acumen but for the fact that he is the owner of the *Washington Post*, a newspaper that regularly calls out Trump.

But then I read about Bezos, who is not far short of being one of the richest men in the world (net worth around US$80 billion) putting on hold an initiative in Seattle that would have helped build houses for homeless families.

Apparently, to help Seattle's homeless, the local council planned to tax Amazon and other big companies in the area, putting the money into a fund to build low-cost houses. According to an article in Curbed, the tax would only apply to businesses making over US$20 million per year and would begin in 2019 as an hours tax. Businesses affected would pay an additional 26 cents per hour for each employee working in Seattle. Eventually, by 2021, the hours tax would be eliminated and replaced with a 0.7% payroll tax, so those businesses would be paying more on higher-salary positions. Both the hour and the payroll tax are expected to raise around US$75 million a year.

Shame on you, Mr Bezos.

On further investigation I discovered that he has never appeared on the Philanthropy 50, the list of America's largest donors. Neither has he created a personal foundation for making charitable gifts.

He is the only one of the top five billionaires in America who has not signed up to Bill Gates and Warren Buffett's 'Giving Pledge', an organisation set up so the super-rich can give away at least half of their wealth. After all, how much money does one man or woman need in their lifetime?

You can't force someone to be philanthropic but as in any aspect of leadership, there will always be people who show how something can and should be done.

So I looked up the world's top philanthropists via the 'Generosity Index', which not only shows how much people have given away, but what percentage of their wealth that represents. Chuck Feeney, an American retail magnate, has actually given away 100% of his worth.

Michael Bloomberg has a net worth of US$37.7 billion and has given away 8% of his worth.

Bill Gates worth is US$84.2 billion and he has given away 32% of his worth.

George Soros has a worth of US$24.4 billion and has given away 33% of his worth.

Warren Buffett's wealth is US$61 billion, having given away 35% of his worth.

Ted Turner has a net worth of US$2.1 billion and has given away 57% of his worth.

But the top prize for philanthropy goes to Sulaiman bin Abdul Aziz Al Rajhi, who has given away 966% of his worth, leaving him with a balance of US$590 million.

And Jeff Bezos can't even see his way to donating 26 cents per hour for each of his Seattle employees.

> *'A little niceness goes a long way. It's a shame that a little meanness goes a lot further.'*
> — Not known

PART V

A THIRST FOR CHANGE

'I just wish that every responsible and concerned person would step back regardless of race and gender and take a closer look at what's really going on in the world today, and say enough is enough.'
— Lonnie Earl Johnson

12

THE PLANET IS CRYING OUT FOR LEADERS TO PLAY THE LONG GAME

'Infinite growth of material consumption in a finite world is an impossibility.'
— E.F. Schumacher, British economist

Short-term gratification versus long-term regret

In August 2017, McKinsey & Company released a paper 'The case against corporate short termism' where they published their findings of a 14-year study of numerous companies that were willing to forfeit short-term gains for long-term sustainability. The full study is published in the Corporate Horizon Index. They discovered that for the firms they identified that focused on the long term, average revenue and earnings growth were 47% more on average by 2014 even factoring in the global financial collapse. They estimate that the US GDP over the past decade might well have grown by an additional US$1 trillion if the whole economy had performed to the same level as their sample companies. They proved that shareholders in the long-term firms would have had a greater return on their investments.

For those business leaders who are charged with or are under pressure to focus only on their next quarter's results, quality could be compromised, customer service will probably become secondary and long-term survival may actually be threatened.

For leaders in the movie sector or music industry who feel compelled to focus only on their 'ratings', they will almost inevitably revert to short-term decisions rather than investing in long-term strategies.

As for politicians who watch only their 'polls' while forgetting what they stand for and why people voted for them, then they will start to appear indecisive and ultimately untrustworthy.

Shareholders have a responsibility in short-term thinking also. If all shareholders care about is a fast return on their investment, then they too are complicit in the potential long-term damage that could be caused to people, communities and/or the environment.

The urgent need for leaders to become futurists

While so many of our leaders are behaving like managers, i.e. managing the day-to-day of a business or country, they are avoiding or delaying or failing to realise that their job, their role and their responsibility is to actually look at the road ahead; to prepare people for what is coming. They employ people to manage the day-to-day.

Leaders need to be educators.

If ever the world needed our leaders to join forces globally and to start preparing their followers for the future rather than encouraging them to hang on to an outdated past, it is now.

We are facing challenges on a global scale like nothing humans have ever faced before, and if we don't start taking urgent action on some of those issues, then this planet could be at risk.

The cost of ignoring early warning signs

As early as the 1940s, a product called DDT (dichlorodiphenyltrichloroethane) was being used in agriculture to rid crops of pests, but which proved toxic to fish and birds. In a report called 'Oceans release DDT from decades ago' by Richard A. Lovett, it is estimated that even though its use was banned in the 1970s, its effect are still being felt in our oceans today.

Why did we not learn from that? And why are we still not learning?

Factoring in costs versus benefits

In 1990 the cod population of Newfoundland was decimated by 'drag' fishing. For a few years the results would have been amazing and shareholder returns would have been very healthy. Sadly, the end result was not just the total depletion of fish stocks, but the loss of 40,000 jobs in five different provinces, which ended up requiring several billion dollars in relief packages.

Having fished out their own waters, the Chinese now have around 2600 vessels that trawl distant waters. As they fish in West Africa, these boats are so large that they can catch in one week what the local Sengalese fisherman would have fished in one year. The cost to the West African economy is estimated to be around US$2 billion.

As early as 1970, concerns around over-fishing caused the introduction of 'catch shares' and has spread to 40 countries. Catch shares mean just that — a quota system which ensures long-term sustainability of fish stocks for people whose livelihood is fishing; for communities where the fishing sector is their main source of jobs and revenue, but more importantly, to prevent the total collapse of fishing stock for future generations. In Iceland, New Zealand and Australia, catch share programmes have now become the default management system for protecting stocks; sadly, this practice didn't reach Newfoundland in time.

So if globally we are finally facing a massive rethink about fishing stocks, perhaps it is also urgently becoming time to look at other resources we are in danger of destroying forever by the short-term pillage of natural resources. Many cities around the world face diminishing supplies of drinking water and massively polluted air quality.

Water: the gold of the future?

Cape Town faced shutting off water to four million people in 2018. Another 11 cities are on the brink of running out of water: San Paulo, Bangalore, Beijing, Cairo, Jakarta, Moscow, Istanbul, Mexico City, London, Tokyo and Miami.

Rapid growth in China is estimated to have lifted 400 million people out of extreme poverty yet in 1997, the World Bank published a 'Clear Water Blue Skies' report where they estimated the economic implications of China's growth and the effect on their environment is costing between 3.5 and 8% of GDP via water and air degradation.

An ever-growing human population is putting stresses on our natural resources like never before. The world population in

1940 was around 2.3 billion, in 2017 the population was 7.6 billion, so it isn't difficult to understand that feeding this ever-growing number of humans has become an immense problem.

Farming requires enormous amounts of chemical fertilisers, which leach into underground water bores. Ancient sewerage systems in many of our bigger cities which were never designed to cope with such massive population growth similarly leach all manner of pollutants into waterways.

Tragically, many of the world's natural waterways now contain water that is undrinkable.

Even though water covers 70% of the Earth's surface, only 3% of that water is actually fresh water and according to UN-endorsed projections, global demand for fresh water will exceed supply by 40% in 2030, thanks to a combination of climate change, human action — or should that be inaction — and population growth.

Some of the world's rivers are so polluted as to be unrecognisable as rivers.

More than a billion gallons of waste every day pours into the Ganges: 75% of this is raw sewage and domestic waste. The balance comes from the industrial runoff from factories and tanneries, all of which leak extremely toxic substances into the river. And yet this river is still used for irrigation and daily home use.

The Pasig River in Manila is so heavily polluted that it has been declared biologically dead. No life is able to survive in its waters — no fish, no plants, nothing.

The Citarum River in Jakarta is similarly so heavily polluted that dead fish dot the surface. Many fishermen have given up their trade and instead harvest plastic waste from the surface to recycle.

In May 2014, residents of Flint, a small town in Michigan, began complaining about water quality. Eventually, researchers discovered that lead levels in the water were at more than double the amount at which water is considered dangerous. Yet even though the results showed these dangerous levels of lead, the Department of Environmental Quality continued to deny that lead polluted water.

In September 2015, Dr Mona Hanna-Attisha conducted her own study, which suggested significant increases of lead in the blood of the children living there. The state government attacked her findings and claimed she was causing hysteria.

In February 2018, Trump signed a bill which means coal companies can now dump mining debris in streams, and on 12 March 2018, the Florida state legislature decided that it was okay for companies to dump treated sewage into local aquifers.

Mining madness

Since the 1990s, coal companies have literally blasted the tops off the Appalachian mountaintops in West Virginia, Kentucky, Virginia and Tennessee. These beautiful peaks, which took hundreds of millions of years to form, are blasted into oblivion in a matter of months. Forests are chopped down and burned. The Environmental Protection Agency predicted that by 2012, 20 years of removing and destroying these mountaintops will have degraded more than 1000 miles of streams.

The more recent practice of fracking (injecting fluid into the ground to break rock and access underlying fossil fuels) is causing damage beyond belief.

Scientific research suggests that fracking can actually cause earthquakes when:

- The fluid injection process occurs in proximity to pre-

existing faults
- Fracking wastewater is disposed of via underground injection.

Fracking is now known to cause various health challenges to people, animals and fish. Water becomes contaminated with radioactive material and potential carcinogens. In Australia, a government report into drilling sites found that half of the gas well heads tested were leaking methane gas.

The practice has been banned or suspended in many places: France, Quebec, Pittsburgh, Buffalo and the Karoo region of South Africa. I'm ashamed to say that New Zealand isn't one of them. The EU has proposed a moratorium while investigation is carried out. Moratoria are in place in New South Wales and New York State.

The National Toxics Network in Australia has called on state and federal governments to introduce, as a matter of urgency, a moratorium on all drilling and fracking chemicals until they have been examined independently.

It is even doubtful that fracking offers much by way of energy returns. David Hughes, a Canadian geologist, suggests that 'Unconventional fossil fuels all share a host of cruel and limiting traits; they consume extreme and endless flows of capital, they provide difficult or volatile rates of supply over time and have large environmental impacts in their extraction.'

It apparently takes between three and nine million gallons of water to extract the oil. The bad news is that this water can only be used once; it is then unusable for any other purpose.

The additional fear is that using these quantities of water could deplete aquifers and cause underground wells to go dry.

There is a thought that the solution to polluted rivers is to 'dilute' the poisons. The problem with that thought is, what would we end up drinking or bathing in? We really do have only one planet and we really must start taking care of it.

Breathe in, breathe out

If water quality and shortages don't terrify us enough, we need to factor in the quality of the air we now get to breathe in our major cities.

Over the years we have seen Chinese cities besieged by air pollution. Eight major cities in China have air quality that is deemed hazardous, and another eight have air quality that is considered very unhealthy.

But Chinese cities pale by comparison to the air pollution in Delhi. In 2014, according to the World Health Organization, Delhi was the most polluted area in the world. Not something to be proud of.

Cities you would not want to linger in because of air quality: Lagos, Nigeria or Delhi; Beijing, Karachi, Pakistan and Los Angeles. These are all cities with the world's worst air quality, according to a new analysis of four major gases associated with air pollution: ammonia, formic acid, methanol, and ozone.

The plastic dilemma

According to EcoWatch, in 10 short years the ocean could contain one ton of plastic for every three tons of fish. They have highlighted the five countries that account for 60% of plastic pollution in oceans: China, Indonesia, the Philippines, Thailand and Vietnam. Tragically, they also estimate that plastic consumption in Asia will increase by an astonishing 80% to surpass 200 million tons.

Some messes may be impossible to clean up

A 2003 National Health Survey discovered that two thirds of the population of China has no access to piped water. This causes diarrhoeal disease to which children under five are particularly vulnerable. The report goes on to suggest that roughly 11% of cancer of the digestive system could be attributed to polluted drinking water.

Even the Antarctic is being affected. For some reason it was hoped that the plastic pollution would never reach these pristine waters, though how anyone could think that I'm not sure — pollution spreads, plastic spreads. Chris Bowler, one of the environmental scientists collecting plankton samples in this area, stated that 'the fact that we found these plastics is a sign that the reach of human beings is truly planetary in scale.'

Our future is coming, ready or not

It is hard to believe that with all the evidence around us, there are still some people who refuse to believe in climate change.

Elon Musk is quoted as saying that 'the future of humanity is going to bifurcate in two directions: either it's going to become multiplanetary, or it's going to remain confined to one planet and eventually there's going to be an extinction event'.

Possibly in generations ahead of us we may have the technology to move to other planets; I just hope we treat them better than we have treated this one. Meanwhile, this is the planet we have, it is all we have, and if we don't remove our blinkers, if we keep polluting and abusing her natural resources, then that extinction event will be our own doing.

> *'Environmental pollution is an incurable disease. It can only be prevented.'*
> — Barry Commoner

13

THE FIGHTBACK HAS BEGUN

'It is at this point, when fear is gone, that whole nations say no. And it is when tyrants fall.'
— Albert Camus

A giant wake-up call

In the case of business leaders, I think they have made massive progress to being more ethical and more conscious of what they do, how they do it and what they say. Business leaders today are moved out really quickly if they prove to be unworthy of the values of their organisation. One scandal hitting the press and businesses now have no hesitation instantly to address the problem or remove the offending person.

Roseanne Barr, star of the very popular sitcom *Roseanne,* sent out a racist tweet on 28 May and within hours ABC had pulled her incredibly popular TV programme. Shortly thereafter, her promoter refused to represent her any longer.

ABC'S parent company is Disney, and Bob Iger, the CEO, immediately apologised saying that he has 'zero tolerance for that sort of racist, bigoted comment.'

Barr went on to make numerous apologies and suggested that her comments were as a result of taking the drug Ambien. This led to a very prompt tweet from the company that makes the drug saying 'racism is not a known side effect [of Ambien]'.

All in the space of hours. The show brought in an estimated US$45 million of advertising revenue for ABC this year, and the network likely would have collected more than US$60 million next season, with the hope of attracting up to US$9 billion in advertising commitments by summer's end.

The target of the hateful tweet was Valerie Jarrett, an African American woman who had served as senior adviser to Barack Obama during his term as POTUS. Speaking at an MSNBC town hall gathering just after the tweet came out, Jarrett suggested that America could use what had just happened as a teaching moment. Her hope was that all Americans would take time to explore their views on race; to really think about the fear and divide that the Trump agenda was promoting with regard to racial differences. In other words — she took the high ground.

Roseanne, however, got a huge wake-up call and it has probably destroyed her career forever. ABC got a wake-up call and responded by pulling the programme despite the huge financial loss. In this case, their reputation was worth more than their revenue. As it should be.

So amid all this chaos the world and America in particular is experiencing, perhaps it is time that our politicians need a wake-up call. Even though they are elected by us, and paid by us, they seem to think they have the right to behave like children; to scoff at anyone who disagrees with them or thinks differently to them; to squander taxpayer money on themselves; to stop listening and caring the second they are elected. They don't have that right. I believe politicians are probably among the last of the old boy networks that need to have a mirror held against their outdated and entrenched behaviours.

Could that one tweet have caused the pendulum to finally start swinging away from the hate and racism and division?

When you see an opportunity to make a difference, don't miss the moment

Dame Anita Roddick once famously said that if we fear that one small thing can't make a difference, we should go to bed with a mosquito. And so it is with any movement, large or small. If someone sees an injustice and is determined to call it out, then mountains are moved.

The women's movement is reborn

Women were the first people to stand up to Trump. They marched the day after the election. It seems that every now and again women have their own 'Enough is enough' periods and go on the march. For any young woman reading this, these are some of the more famous of them:

1867 The London Society for Women's Suffrage is formed.

1870 The Married Women's Property Act allows married women to own their own property. Previously, when women married, their property transferred to their husbands. Divorce heavily favoured men, allowing property to remain in their possession. This act allowed women to keep their property, whether married, divorced, single or widowed.

19 September 1893 New Zealand became the first self-governing country in the world in which all women had the right to vote in parliamentary elections.

1918 Women over 30 are granted the right to vote in Britain.

1920 The UK Sex Discrimination Removal Act allows women access to the legal profession and accountancy.

1941 The National Service Act is passed introducing conscription for women. All unmarried women between the ages of 20 and 30 are called up for war work. It is later extended to include women up to age 43 and married women, though pregnant women and those with young children can be exempt.

1948 The introduction of the National Health Service (NHS) gives everyone free access to health care. Previously, only the insured, usually men, benefited.

1968 Women at the Ford car factory in Dagenham strike over equal pay, almost stopping production at all Ford UK plants. Their protest led directly to the passing of the Equal Pay Act.

It was with awe and amazement then that I watched the sheer speed and passion of the women who mobilised and voiced their concerns about Donald Trump becoming the President of the USA in January 2017. The day after his inauguration, women all over the world were marching against his style of leadership.

Actress America Ferrera told the women who had gathered that 'We march today for the moral core of this nation, against which our new president is waging a war.' She went on to say 'Our dignity, our character, our rights have all been under attack, and a platform of hate and division assumed power yesterday. But the President is not America. We are America, and we are here to stay.'

Ashley Judd took on Harvey Weinstein loudly and publicly when he tried to molest her in a hotel room. Judd escaped but rather than stay silent, she marched straight down to the reception area of the hotel where her father was waiting for her, and she spoke up. She told her father and she told everyone and anyone she could.

Weinstein's hideous and long-running game was over.

And so a tidal wave was launched. We've already talked about the #MeToo movement when we met Tarana Burke in Chapter 1; #MeToo led to her big sister, the #TimesUp movement. Started by over 300 women in Hollywood, high-profile leaders like Reese Witherspoon, Natalie Portman and Shonda Rhimes took on the male-based culture of Hollywood, their belief being that every human being deserves the right to earn a living, to take care of their families and to be free of harassment, sexual assault and discrimination.

This in turn led to the TIME'S UP Legal Defense Fund being launched. Housed and administered by the National Women's Law Center, they will connect any woman who has experienced sexual misconduct with legal and public relations assistance. The fund will help defray costs based on availability of funds; US$21 million was raised in just two months.

And so all of these resistance movements led to *Time* magazine naming 'The Silence Breakers' as Person of the Year; they made the women who had stood up and spoken up the stars of 2017.

The nominees for Person of the Year were no slouches:

- Jeff Bezos (Amazon CEO)
- The Dreamers (undocumented children of immigrants)
- Patty Jenkins (director of *Wonder Woman*, a female-driven box office success story)
- Kim Jong-un (North Korean leader)
- Colin Kaepernick (NFL player who started the 'kneeling' movement)
- The #MeToo movement (women denouncing sexual assault

and harassment)
- Robert Mueller (head of Special Counsel investigating Russian collusion)
- Mohammed bin Salman (Crown Prince of Saudi Arabia)
- Donald Trump (POTUS)
- Xi Jinping (President of China)

So in less than a year of Trump becoming POTUS, women who had probably been silent for years about all manner of abuse, suddenly decided en masse that 'Enough was enough'. They named and shamed bosses, TV hosts and elected officials for all manner of sexual harassment.

Black American women took down Roy Moore, the Republican candidate accused of historical sexual misconduct with young girls. They went out in force to vote; 98% of black women in Alabama voted for Doug Jones, the Democratic candidate. In his victory speech Doug Jones said: 'This entire race has been about dignity and respect ... This campaign has been about the rule of law; about common courtesy and decency and making sure everyone in this state, regardless of which zip code you live in, is going to get a fair shake in life.'

John Carman, the Republican candidate in the November 2017 elections who famously and patronisingly said, 'Will the Women's March protest be over in time for them to cook dinner?' was beaten by a woman.

Robert Marshall, who proudly called himself the 'Chief Homophobe', was beaten by Danica Roem, the first transgender to be elected to office.

Nikki Haley, the US Ambassador to the UN, courageously took the bull by the horns when she said, 'The time has come to start bringing a conscience to the situation surrounding the treatment of women in the workplace as well as on Capitol Hill.' Which was incredibly brave given that her boss (Trump) has so many women claiming he sexually harassed them.

It wasn't just women saying enough.

Colin Kaepernick started a movement with the American NFL players when he refused to stand for the national anthem and instead kneeled down as a protest against police brutality against African Americans. The process took off as others across the code also 'took the knee' during the national anthem.

The fightback for transgenders: Trump's administration is trying desperately to ban transgender people from serving in the military, and to remove the existing transgender personnel. However, four federal judges have recently refused to pass the bill.

Jeff Flake, a Republican Senator, is choosing to leave politics because, in his words:

> 'Reckless, outrageous, and undignified behaviour has become excused and countenanced as "telling it like it is", when it is actually just reckless, outrageous, and undignified. And when such behaviour emanates from the top of our government, it is something else: it is dangerous to a democracy. Such behaviour does not project strength — because our strength comes from our values. It instead projects a corruption of the spirit, and weakness.' He went on to say: 'It is often said that children are watching. Well, they are. And what are we going to do about that?' He also worried about what to say when the next generation asks us, 'Why didn't you do something? Why didn't you speak up?' 'What are we going to say? Mr President, I rise today to say: Enough.'

Name and shame movements rising to the surface

It seems that a whole raft of society has had enough of all the terrible behaviours we are witnessing from our so-called leaders, whether they be politicians or business leaders.

In the UK a list of 233 businesses have been named and shamed for failing to pay their workers the minimum wage. These employers have been fined an additional £1.9 million. The worst offenders were retail, hairdressing and hospitality, and since the inception of this initiative in 2013, the scheme has forced bad bosses to pay out a total of £6 million in back pay for some 40,000 workers.

Australia names and shames food outlets via a food register. Outlets as famous as Domino's Pizza, KFC and Gloria Jean's coffee shops have been issued penalties for unsafe food practices. Since the register was set up, over 7000 food outlets have been named and publicly shamed.

The EU creates a black list of tax havens and puts them on notice: 17 countries have been named and another 47 put on notice; Jersey, Guernsey and the Isle of Man have been warned. The blacklist also includes South Korea, Mongolia, Namibia, Panama, Bahrain and the UAE.

Jim Yong Kim, President of the World Bank, has warned that he will name and shame countries that fail to tackle the challenges of malnourishment. He has promised to take the stand at the World Economic Forum in Davos and call out governments that fail to live up to the promises they make.

The climate change movement gathers momentum

Glasgow University becomes the first university in Europe to divest from fossil fuels. The movement actually began in US campuses and has caused US$50 billion worth of divestments moved away from fossil fuels. According to Fossil Free, 837 institutions have so far moved away from carbon fuels and the rate of signing up has apparently doubled since 2014.

Bill McKibben, environmentalist and figurehead for the movement, was quoted as saying 'Here's my bet: the kids are going to win, and when they do, it's going to matter.'

The great news

Slowly but surely we are watching various people and groups around the world waking up, standing up and speaking up. All over the world, people are saying their version of 'Enough' to the power-hungry leaders hellbent on destruction.

Some countries refused to sell off or sabotage various waterways for short-term profits.

The Tara River runs through Montenegro, Bosnia and Herzegovina. It wends its way through mountains and even forms the Tara River Canyon, now a recognised World Heritage Site; the water is so clean that you can drink from it. This crystal-clear water wasn't achieved without fierce opposition from locals who prevented several attempts to build dams along the river.

Ireland also has worked long and hard to ensure the Caragh River is protected under a national law for conservation.

And if ever there was an environmental success story, it is the River Thames in London. For years the river was so polluted that it too was declared biologically dead. It wasn't unknown for people who lived alongside the river to die from cholera. The UK government stepped in and took action. Factories were banned from dumping pollution into the river and water treatment plants were built along its course. Slowly the river recovered and is now regarded as the cleanest river in the world that flows through a major city.

So if one city can clean up its water supplies, others can too. As in the case of the River Thames, it doesn't happen overnight — it took 50 years to clean it up. Starting the process required strong leadership; it required the whole community to get in behind the vision. It also required a strong determination that any business that tries to get round legislation for dumping toxic materials in the river will be dealt with severely.

Finally, China is seriously tackling its air pollution. In 2013 it implemented a nationwide cap on coal usage. Beijing, for example, had to reduce consumption by 50% in five years — 2013 to 2018.

China and India are both embracing solar power. Rajasthan has the world's largest solar project under construction, and China has commissioned the world's largest floating solar project.

Germany is now working on a plan to make public transport free in its biggest and most polluted cities. Yes, they were pressured into the action by the EU, but if that is what it takes, then good on the EU.

Finland has a goal of ensuring 38% of its energy comes from renewable sources by 2020 and has made this target legally binding.

Meanwhile, and tragically, the USA is going backwards with regard to looking after its environment and even in its unwillingness to address the factual evidence that climate change is real.

Fortunately, Michael Bloomberg, former New York mayor and billionaire, has promised to write a check for US$4.5 million to cover this year's payments towards the Paris climate agreement.

The amazing news

Sweden has turned a major problem into an amazing business opportunity. In 1991, and well in advance of most other developed nations, Sweden put a tax on fossil fuels. Heating is a major challenge for the country so they set up plants to incinerate garbage and to distribute that power directly into district heating systems without the need to transform it into electricity.

They became so good at doing this that they decided to import rubbish from other countries; a great idea. However, they didn't 'purchase' the rubbish, they instead charged countries for the service. So they won on both counts: heat and revenue being generated from garbage.

The Netherlands closed down 19 prisons in 2013 and plan to close five more — they don't have enough prisoners to justify keeping them open. They helped Norway out by taking 240 of their prisoners just to keep the facilities functioning. They achieved this magnificent outcome with a combination of relaxing drug laws, putting time and resources into rehabilitation rather than incarceration, and an ankle monitoring system which allows people to either keep working or re-enter the workforce. The country has a population of 17 million and only 11,600 prisoners, which equates to 69 incarcerations per 100,000, versus America's rate of 716 per 100,000. (America, with the highest rate in the world, gives little or no attention to social services or rehabilitation once people complete their sentences.) They plan also to turn those empty prisons into homes for refugees.

A Norwegian billionaire, once a fisherman, plans to give away the majority of his US$2.6 billion fortune in a bid to help clean up the world's oceans. Kjell Inge Røkke, once described in *Forbes* magazine as a 'ruthless corporate raider', wants to build a 596-foot marine research ship that will scour the seas scooping up plastic litter.

Mushrooms will hopefully replace plastic in the not too distant future. Ecovative is a company that was started nine years ago and doubles in size every year. Based in Green Island, New York, the company has licensed its process for mushroom packaging to Sealed Air, a US$7.6 billion international packaging supplier traditionally known for bubble wrap. Other large companies like Dell Computers, Puma and Ikea are showing an interest in the product.

Six years ago, Dutch teen prodigy Boyan Slat presented his ocean-cleaning machine at a TEDx talk. It will be used to clean up what has become known as 'the great Pacific garbage patch', a massive chunk of ocean plastic halfway between California and Hawaii, estimated to be 1.8 trillion pieces of plastic rubbish amassed there by ocean currents. Basically, the machine is a giant tube that will suck the plastic waste out of the water and then transfer it to large ships, which will then take the waste to shore for recycling.

Initially, Slat raised US$2.2 million from a crowdfunding campaign; with millions more brought in by other investors, the project is now backed by a Dutch not-for-profit organisation with the aim of installing 60 giant floating scoops, each stretching a mile from end to end.

Roger Federer has donated US$13.5 million to open 81 schools in Africa; he has already invested in 80 preschools there and it is estimated that he will change the lives of 150,000 Malawian children by 2021.

How a 'Youthquake' is showing up apathetic leaders

Many countries around the world are experiencing what has been described as a 'Youthquake'.

I'd heard rumblings that the youth of North Korea were quietly starting to rebel, but all my Google searches came to naught with the exception of one extract I briefly found from a book *The Impossible State: North Korea, past and future* where suggestions that a 'contagion' effect could cause their young people to say

'Enough'. Literally hours after I found it, all mention of this book had been removed from the internet.

Teenagers at Parkland School in Florida may just be creating the biggest gun backlash America has seen since the Civil Rights movement. They are standing up to politicians and the National Rifle Association with courage and determination. Far from being cowed or intimidated by the NRA, they are showing a leadership that every single American should be proud of.

Hopefully, after the turbulence of 2017, we have all had enough of abuse and bullying and passing the buck from people who should know better and be better. Hopefully, we will all have the courage to stand up or kneel, whichever is appropriate, if we witness behaviours that go against basic human values; actions that risk wars and decisions that risk the planet. Hopefully in 2018, we will all have the courage to say to our leaders, shape up or ship out.

The only way is up

J.K. Rowling once said that rock bottom became the solid foundation on which she rebuilt her life. If any of us at any stage of our lives have hit our own rock bottom because of a broken marriage or the loss of a job or being made bankrupt or being diagnosed with a debilitating health crisis, whatever, then at some point we will realise that like J.K. Rowling, the only way now is up.

I wonder if Donald Trump could not only be America's rock bottom, but also the planet's rock bottom. If so, then his tumultuous presidency will have served a purpose. It will have shown American people that division, chaos and abuse serves no-one; and that as a global population, we have some bigger battles ahead than personal vendettas and party political pettiness if we want to actually have a planet to live on.

We surely have to start factoring in the damage that we as humans are causing to this beautiful planet and because we have no idea what 'rock bottom' really is, or at what point we can no longer save the planet, that doesn't mean that we keep polluting until it's too late. Surely?

The Paris Agreement: 118 nations ratified this agreement in 2016 to ensure a unified global strategy to tackle climate change. The only country in the world that has pulled out is the USA under Donald Trump; every other country, including Syria, is part of the agreement.

Earth Day was actually the idea of John McConnell, newspaper publisher and community activist. He proposed the idea of a global holiday called 'Earth Day' at a UNESCO conference in 1969. The aim was to remind people of the shared responsibility of caring for the planet.

US Senator and environmental activist Gaylord Nelson picked up the idea and mobilised people and organisations to get in behind the initiative.

The goal of Earth Day 2018 is to focus on changing the human attitudes to plastic and plastic pollution. If each one of us made just one small change to how we live our lives with regard to plastic, we could make such an impact. In business, if supermarkets simply changed their bags from plastic to paper and stopped wrapping fruit and vegetables in plastic, those simple steps would have such a huge impact on the environment.

> *'Earth Day achieved what I had hoped for and then some. The purpose of Earth Day was to get a nationwide demonstration of concern for the environment so large that it would shake the political establishment out of its lethargy and, finally, force this issue permanently into the political arena. Having criss-crossed the nation speaking on environmental issues during the previous eight or nine years it was dear to me that the public was far ahead of*

the politicians and given an opportunity they would demonstrate their interest. It was a gamble but it worked. It got the attention of the politicians. An estimated twenty million people participated in peaceful demonstrations all across the country. Ten thousand schools, two thousand colleges and one thousand communities were involved.'

— Gaylord Nelson

PART VI

THE FOURTH WAVE

'When I look into the future, it's so bright it burns my eyes.'
— Oprah Winfrey

14

GLOBAL CHALLENGES NEED GLOBAL SOLUTIONS

'When I give food to the poor, they call me a saint; when I ask why the poor have no food, they call me a communist.'
— Dom Hélder Câmara

The Third Wave

I'd studied Alvin Toffler's book *The Third Wave* at Auckland University. Toffler identified three periods of the most intense societal disruption the world had experienced over several hundred years.

An Agricultural Age had lasted for centuries; people had lived and worked on the land for generations. In the mid 1700s the first signs of the Industrial Age appeared. Britain had a natural supply of coal, iron and waterways and started using water as a source of power via watermills. Power and water led to the birth of steam engines and so began all manner of inventions leading to the building of factories, automation and mass production.

Suddenly, people who had worked on the land and were paid annually — and even then only if the crops were successful — were lured to work in those early factories on the never-before-heard-of promise of weekly wages.

The first computers came along in the 1930s and led the world into the Age of Technology, which took mass production to a whole realm of output. That age is now actually challenging the very jobs that were created in factories as more and more mass production is managed by robotics.

As society passed from one age to the next, traditional jobs vanished or were dramatically changed. Wage earners who had planned on a job for life in some way, shape or form were invariably caught unprepared and untrained for the new opportunities that were created as technology took over most repetitive tasks.

Given time, of course, change simply becomes the new way we did things; younger people adapt and older people sadly find themselves under-skilled, grumpy and unemployed unless they choose differently.

From an American perspective, the discord that Trump has sown could be a major tipping point in where America goes next: backwards or forwards?

Lawrence Wright, author of *God Save Texas: A journey into the future of America,* describes the current mood of America as the politics of resentment; that it isn't so much the workers who are feeling disenfranchised, rather it is that older white men are feeling despised. Because he is a Texan, he was mystified at voters there on election day. There are 29 million mostly Hispanic residents of Texas, 19 million of whom are registered to vote, and yet only nine million actually did vote. So whether that was because they didn't like either of the candidates, his point was, imagine if 19 million Hispanics in his state were mobilised to vote for the future they wanted in Texas for their children and grandchildren.

If this rise of non-whites across America actually gathers momentum, what then?

Back to those Parkland kids again: not content with just taking on the NRA, these kids, led by young David Hogg, are mobilising students to get out and vote for the first time. They have been taking on any senators who are funded by or who support the NRA; their aim is to cause a blue (Democratic) wave to hit America in the mid-term elections, particularly in some of the marginal seats.

So many problems, so many ways to avoid facing them

I'd spent over 30 years helping organisations and people with change, and I have my own personal concerns for what the future holds for my grandchildren.

I personally worry about climate change; whole countries emptying and other countries overflowing; the rich getting richer while the poor are getting poorer; having the technology to heal most medical problems but people not being able to afford to have the treatment; a never-ending growth in population that must be straining every resource this planet has. I also worry about the enormous amount of money being spent on weapons of mass destruction and not enough money being put into education and social services.

So when I investigated what other people worry about, I

discovered via the World Economic Forum (WEF) that the top three challenges they discovered in their surveys were:

- Food security. The estimate is that by 2050 we must be able to feed 9.7 billion people.
- Job opportunities. The International Labour Organization has watched over 61 million jobs vanish since the global financial crisis in 2008. More than 200 million people are unemployed globally.
- Climate change. Global greenhouse gas emissions have grown by 80% since 1970, the highest level in 800,000 years.

The WEF conducted a further study asking what millennials were concerned about given that 50% of the world's population is under 30. Their challenges were slightly different:

- Climate change was top of their list.
- Concern for large-scale conflicts.
- Inequality.

We still don't appear to have any cohesive global solutions to food crises, immigration challenges, inequity, social services, health and education and the ever-widening gap between rich and poor. We just seem to muddle along as a human race, moving from one crisis to the next, focusing on the now rather than the future, putting sticking plasters on things we don't want to have to deal with or invest in, pouring vast resources into all the wrong things, and tolerating despots and tyrants who on a whim or bad hair day could blow us all to kingdom come.

The forum concludes that none of the above challenges can be solved by any one country — we really are all in this together, we really do have only one planet — and while Elon Musk suggests we need to think intergalactically, for now, this one planet is all we have for the moment. As Richard Branson famously said, 'There is no planet B.'

Fortunately, just as there are people who are willing to avoid making decisions or fixing things that need fixing, heroes do come to the fore just when we absolutely need them.

Technology: our greatest weapon, our greatest fear

When a tweet can reach millions in seconds, we all have to be aware of the damage that can do to personal reputations and business credibility. A company's reputation can be destroyed overnight; a person's career can be trashed in the blink of an eye; a country leader can be shown up as out of control; a war could be started because of a childish insult.

But technology is also causing waves of a different kind.

The McKinsey Global Institute has estimated that 800 million jobs will be lost by 2030 because of the advances in technology. But it isn't all bad news, because new jobs are being created daily, as a result of technology. The report suggests that approximately 5% of current occupations will be totally wiped out, while other positions will be enhanced by technology automating the more tedious parts of a job and freeing up human time to do more productive things.

If you 'google' jobs for 2030 you will find an array of possibilities. All manner of energy jobs are being created to replace fossil fuels, and given the massive population, all things food related, including organic farming.

The hierarchy will be further flattened. More managerial positions, more project management jobs, more lower skilled jobs in harvesting and manual labour that simply can't be done by robots or AI.

Research firm Gartner predicts that by 2020, AI will generate more than two million jobs; slightly more than the 1.8 million it will remove. They predict that healthcare and education will be the winners while manufacturing and transportation will be the losers. Gartner suggests that 'Robots are not here to take our jobs, they're here to give us a promotion.'

And if the worst (or best) case scenario eventuates that we don't need so many humans to work at all, imagine the possibilities of people choosing not to work but rather taking a universal income could make.

Ontario is trialling just such an idea. Unemployed people or those on a low income can receive up to C$17,000 plus still keep half of what they earn if they want to work — this way they earn a living income but still have an incentive to contribute in some way to their community and to even aid their mental health. Depression is a huge side effect of losing a job and not being able to find a replacement one.

Kathleen Wynne, Premier of Ontario, shared her experience of going to a factory where a machine had replaced 20 people and realised they had to plan for this eventuality for society going forward.

One recipient from the Canadian trial says that the extra C$750 a month he receives has helped him to cope with the mental illness that has kept him out of work since 2002, and that he hopes to find work helping others with mental health challenges.

Similarly, a Canadian security guard who fell from a roof and was unable to work again is delighted that the basic income has taken the worry and stress off him to be able to pay his rent and food, which in turn has lifted his depression and given him a new lease on life.

Stockton, California, has its fair share of challenges post the housing bust. Homeless people now live in tents along railroad tracks. The town is the picture of depression: boarded-up shop fronts, cracked roads and pavements, and an increase in gang violence.

The plan to donate US$500 per month to around a hundred families with no strings attached is being set up as a trial. I just hope some support structures are put around the families to help them make the money work for them, which will then hopefully lead to others being given a hand up also.

Finland, Oakland, Hawaii and the Dutch city of Utrecht are all going to trial a similar concept.

The crisis of trust

As I summarise the contents of this book, my greatest fear is that we seem to have lost trust in our leaders.

In politics it has become the norm that one party says one thing and the other party says the opposite. Who do we believe? Who is just playing politics? Who is out and out lying to us? Who is simply telling us what we want to hear while lining their own pockets? Who is spreading fake lies and conspiracies?

It would appear that Trump is doing everything in his power to destroy the credibility of the FBI and the Department of Justice so he can sabotage the Russia investigation. What that is doing to the morale of the hardworking people in those organisations is anyone's guess; the challenge is the years it will take to restore trust in the legal framework of America, which, up until now, has been the backbone of America.

Which takes me back to the chapter on followership.

If something sounds too good to be true, it probably is. People can only fool us if we are too lazy to read or listen or ask questions. If we trust ourselves, and someone is trying to con us, our gut will tell us that something doesn't feel right.

I know whole families who vote a certain way because the family has always voted that way. Just because our sister or husband or mother thinks one way, it doesn't mean that we have to think that way too. We are allowed to have our own thoughts and to make our own decisions and to vote the way we feel is right for us.

Finding a way to deal with the tyrants and despots

> *'What is a rebel? A man who says no. It is at this point, when fear is gone, that whole nations say no. And it is when tyrants fall.'* — Albert Camus

Because of technology and instant news from all manner of sources — some reliable, some quite dangerous — we seem to be experiencing human division on levels unheard of. I'm right, you are wrong; Republican versus Democrat; conservative versus liberal; male versus female; white versus coloured; heterosexual versus homosexual; my religion is better than yours, etc.

Right now the world has its fair share of despots. I guess the world has always had them, it's just that with 24/7 news cycles we can't ignore them as we probably could in the days when news arrived via the town crier.

How do they get into power, why do we let them stay in power, and how do we get them out of power?

As I write this we have the nuclear threat in North Korea; the civil war in Syria being aided and abetted by Russia and Iran; we have the never-ending cyber war being waged by Russia on every democratic nation; we have China beginning to take over as world leader given that Trump has abdicated that role; and we have Erdogan and Duterte up to who knows what.

These out-of-control egos are costing lives and literally risk another global economic meltdown or, at worst, the actual planet being blown into oblivion.

How did it get to be this way? Why do we not have steps or processes that have teeth?

A hundred years ago I imagine the selfsame wars and feuds were being fought; the difference then was that we wouldn't have known about them and despots wouldn't have had the capability to blow the planet to smithereens. News travelled very slowly a hundred years ago. Now we are virtually taken into wars via instant video links. We have a daily diet of bad news and despair.

So over the eons there have been any number of dictators and despots: Genghis Khan, Joseph Stalin, Pol Pot, Idi Amin, Robert Mugabe, to name just a few. All of these men were responsible for the deaths of millions of people, yet some of them remained in power for many years.

Genghis Khan's demise is confusing; he either died as a result of a war injury or was stabbed by a young princess. He reigned from 1206 to 1227, had 12 wives and is discredited with having killed around 40 million people.

Stalin died of old age and a massive stroke after his reign of terror lasted from 1929 to 1953, during which it is estimated he killed 20–25 million people.

Pol Pot died of heart disease at 73 after a fairly short reign, 1975–79, but in that time he managed to kill 1.5–2 million Cambodians through starvation, execution, disease or overwork. The movie *The Killing Fields* is about him.

Idi Amin was overthrown after an eight-year regime when an estimated 300,000 civilians were massacred. He was eventually overthrown by Ugandan and Tanzanian exiles but never brought to trial and lived out the rest of his life in Saudi Arabia. In the short period he was in power, he brought about the country's virtual economic ruin.

Mugabe is still alive and well, though he resigned under pressure from the military after serving for 37 years. He turned Zimbabwe from the fruit bowl of the world, after expelling thousands of white farmers, into what is now a veritable dust bowl. The new leader, Emmerson Mnangagwa, is inviting those exiled white farmers to return and help rebuild their economy.

I'm not suggesting for one second that Trump is even remotely in this category. All I'm suggesting is that power does strange things to people and countries have to find a way to limit the power of the people they have in charge of their countries.

I loved the solution Max Boot, a global affairs analyst, offered when he asked what was to be done to stop Donald Trump from getting even more out of control. He said words to the effect of:

> 'I'm a lifelong Republican and I fear that people in America have faced so many outrages during Trump's term, that they have become numb; the only way to solve this problem is for everyone in America to become a Democrat when they vote in the mid-terms.'

This was a belief also shared by Peter Beaumont, a writer for the *Guardian*, who said, 'Dictatorial regimes, regarded as stable and invulnerable by outside observers, can collapse as quickly as they can, not least when a key element like the military, as happened in Egypt and Tunisia, removed its support.' He went on to say, 'In the end, however, the success of a rebellion depends on the crossing of a fear barrier by enough people, not simply a small group of dedicated dissidents. A judgement that the risk is worth it and the rebellion might actually succeed.'

Championing civility and kinder politics

I'd been speaking at a Rotary event just after Jacinda Ardern was elected our Prime Minister; I was comparing her gentle style of leadership with Donald Trump's bombastic style.

I asked the question, 'Is it possible to have kinder politics?'

There was a very long silence, which for a speaker can be quite terrifying, but I was determined to see what reaction I would get. It was a woman who spoke first. She was actually quite tearful as she said, 'Since Jacinda was elected, for the first time in years, I feel hope. Hope that we don't need this dog-eat-dog way our politicians treat each other which says to my kids it's okay to berate people and rubbish them and abuse them. So if there is even a glimmer of hope that we can have kinder politics, I will be the first to sign up.'

> *'Today, more than ever before, life must be characterised by a sense of Universal responsibility, not only nation to nation and human to human, but also human to other forms of life.'*
> — the Dalai Lama

15

DON'T GIVE UP ON DEMOCRACY

> *'Where you see wrong or inequality or injustice, speak out, because this is your country. This is your democracy. Make it. Protect it. Pass it on.'*
> — Thurgood Marshall

Having worked with teams, couples and families over the years, I know that when a manager or parent or partner asks for help, it's because they truly don't know how to fix whatever problem they are experiencing. And yet I truly have seen miracles happen when people with a problem are willing to risk trying something new, to give something a go; to be willing to acknowledge their part in the problem.

In every team you will quite naturally have different personalities, different skills, different goals and different agendas. If a manager can't bring these people together to focus on a common goal, then all manner of misery, confusion and even conflict can arise.

You can have a team that has functioned perfectly well for a number of years, then one person leaves, a new person joins and the dynamics can very quickly fall apart. The manager has to start from scratch to re-form this new team.

Unifying a team takes time and courage.

Managers have to be willing to state categorically that the goals and values of the team are not negotiable; that personal agendas and factions will not be tolerated. Members of the team must take personal stock and decide if they can live with that. If they can't, then they should make the decision to leave or to decide not to join that team in the first place. Joining and being miserable, or staying and trying to cause dissent are not acceptable options.

So if we realise how challenging it is to unite a team of, say, six or seven people, imagine what it must be like for the leader of a political party or, tougher still, the leader of a country. Imagine the competing goals and agendas. Imagine the challenges of trying to unify hundreds, thousands and even hundreds of thousands of people.

Abraham Lincoln talked about democracy as being government of the people, by the people and for the people, yet so many of our Western democracies seem to be in crisis.

I heard one politician being interviewed on CNN recently and his observations were that in America, the Republicans were focusing on trying to please only the far right of their party and the Democrats were trying to gratify only the far left of theirs.

Think of the millions of ordinary people in the middle of that continuum who are confused, lost, fearful and ignored. So if unifying a small team is daunting, imagine the challenges of uniting a country.

I've always loved the Charles de Gaulle quote 'How can anyone govern a nation that has 246 kinds of cheese?' How do leaders find a way to unify constituencies that want their own demands to be met regardless of any long-term consequences for their communities and even country?

That is a leader's challenge.

Have we as voters become selfish, expecting that our needs will be met to the detriment of other members of society? Have we failed to work out what we will sacrifice as individuals and as countries, for the greater good of the long term?

Could we, instead of complaining about whatever our leaders are doing or not doing, step forward and take some responsibility in our towns or communities if we are not happy with what we see?

A recent Massey University study of New Zealand voters discovered that about half of the people they surveyed were 'discontented'. When you look at the bounty of privileges and freedoms we have here in New Zealand versus, say, North Korea, you have to wonder what is wrong with these people.

So if we are facing an underbelly of discontent with democracy, then we need to stand up and be counted, because not living in a democracy doesn't bear thinking about. We need to get involved instead of sniping from a distance. We need to be willing to realise that no matter our colour or creed, or wealth or station in life, we have to have a middle road that works for the majority.

The fringe dwellers will just have to take their chances.

Charles de Gaulle also said, 'You start out giving your hat, then you give your coat, then your shirt, then your skin and finally your soul.' Politicians have to also stand up and be counted, not just in terms of votes, but in terms of credibility.

I personally want politicians to stop playing politics and do the job that the taxpayer pays them for. I want them to stop undoing everything the previous government did just to make their mark; and I'd dearly love them to stop whinging about any initiative the current government takes — it makes them sound quite pathetic.

Politicians need to learn a new language, and I know that won't be easy. But if they don't, they risk exactly what is happening — people being turned off by their behaviours and not bothering to vote.

I also want voters to stop whining about their lot and get involved in creating the change they want to see.

Pendulums do swing, nothing lasts forever; sooner or later bad times turn into good times if people are willing to stand up for what they believe in, to challenge behaviours they think are not okay, to be willing to be counted, to be willing to be the change they wish to see. Then they will get exactly what they deserve: a true democracy.

Kia kaha, people everywhere

Kia kaha is a Maori phrase which means 'Stay strong'.

Maya Angelou famously said:

> 'You have to develop ways so that you can take up for yourself, and then you take up for someone else. And so sooner or later you have the courage to stand up for the human race and say "I'm a representative."'

I believe that going forward into who knows what, we all need to be strong, and we all need to become 'representatives'.

So whether you are male or female, heterosexual or homosexual, young or old, religious or not, let's each do what we can to take care of our planet, to care about democracy and to treat each other more kindly. Treating people with respect doesn't make us weaker; it actually makes us stronger. It says, I don't necessarily agree with what you say or think, but I accept your right to say that or think that.

If we are seven billion people, then surely we have to learn to understand each other? Surely we have to learn to work together? Surely we need to find a way to look after our nest?

I don't know what the immediate future will bring us as we endure the presidency of Donald Trump; I don't know how his term will end or even when his term will end. But I do know this: as long as he keeps behaving badly, I will keep calling him out.

So in his words, 'Let's see what happens.'

To be continued.

> *'When we least expect it, life sets us a challenge to test our courage and willingness to change. At such a moment there's no point pretending that nothing has happened or in saying we are not ready. The challenge will not wait.'*
> — Paulo Coelho

RECOMMENDED READING

Lessons in Leadership: 50 ways to avoid falling into the 'Trump' trap, Ann Andrews

Built to Last, James C. Collins and Jerry I. Porras

The Third Wave, Alvin Toffler

Ethics in Politics, Benoît Girardin

What Happened, Hillary Clinton

Fire and Fury, Michael Wolff

It's Even Worse Than You Think, David Cay Johnston

The Art of the Deal, Donald Trump

Trump's Brain, Dr Decker (pen name)

The Dangerous Case of Donald Trump, Bandy Lee

A Higher Loyalty, James Comey

Games People Play, Dr Eric Berne

Trump Revealed, Michael Kranish and Marc Fisher

Good to Great, Jim Collins

No, It's Not OK, Tania Roxborogh and Kim Stephenson

The Soul of America, Jon Meacham

War on Peace, Ronan Farrow

God Save Texas, Lawrence Wright

FURTHER RESOURCES

www.bullyonline.org

www.workplace.com

www.bullybusters.org

To download an example of a bullying policy for your workplace go to:

http://www.forbes.com/sites/naomishavin/2014/06/25/what-work-place-bullying-looks-like-in-2014-and-how-to-intervene/

FURTHER READING

https://listverse.com/2012/02/21/10-terrible-decisions-of-the-20th-century/

http://www.cracked.com/pictofacts-356-21-tiny-mistakes-that-changed-history/

https://www.scientificamerican.com/article/the-psychology-of-the-breathtakingly-stupid-mistake/

https://www.weforum.org/agenda/2017/01/8-leadership-lessons-from-history/

https://www.washingtonpost.com/world/national-security/trump-plans-to-ask-for-716-billion-for-national-defense-in-2019–a-major-increase/2018/01/26/9d0e30e4-02a8-11e8-bb03-722769454f82_story.html

ACKNOWLEDGEMENTS

I was pretty much on my own with this book.

My husband and friends had all become a bit 'Trump' weary after my year of writing *Lessons in Leadership: 50 ways to avoid falling into the 'Trump' trap*. They didn't exactly avoid me, but I could sense that they were totally over him and really didn't want to hear about him or even discuss him any longer . And that was totally okay, I understood.

The challenge with including the behaviours of someone who is still in power is that things change so rapidly, so trying to keep up and to keep current is a challenge. Every day I wonder what could possibly happen next that I feel duty bound to include. However, leadership is not time bound. Good leaders are good leaders whether they led in the 1930s or will lead in the 2030s, and ditto for bad leaders. Unless leaders are willing to take responsibility for their style, their results, their mistakes and even their ill-advised strategies, then they will continue to be poor leaders.

This book, then, has been written while quietly shut away in my office.

I've read and followed all the great journalists on the *Washington Post*, the *New York Times*, the *Guardian* and *Huffington Post* on a daily basis. I made great friends with Google 'searches'. Who would have thought you could 'google' 'does power make your brain go stupid' and actually find out that it does?

I watched great interviews and debates on CNN with Anderson Cooper, Wolf Blitzer, Christiane Amanpour, Fareed Zakaria and David Axelrod. I became a great fan of *State of the Union* with Jake Tapper and tried never to miss the hard-hitting news reports and panel discussions with Don Lemon.

One particularly powerful Anderson Cooper interview was with Bob Woodward and Carl Bernstein, the journalists who became the Watergate whistle-blowers, as they discussed the comparison between the Robert Mueller investigation into Russian interference in the 2016 presidential election and the downfall of Richard Nixon. I clearly remember the Watergate crisis and was in awe of the courage of those two men and delighted when their bravery was made into the movie *All the President's Men*.

So this chaotic presidency of Trump became the second era in my lifetime when I watched great journalists step up to the plate and people of courage saying 'This is not okay' no matter the effect on their careers.

For sure, democracy cannot survive when the press is silenced nor when good people fail to call out unacceptable behaviours. So as with my first 'Trump' book, this book is not meant to be just about him; it is a book about leadership.

ABOUT THE AUTHOR

I spent four amazing years in the Women's Royal Navy, mostly working with the Royal Marines. I worked in a rather boring department — pay and records — which is where certain highly trained members of the marines would be stationed as they waited for the call-up to go wherever a conflict situation arose. They were the equivalent of what we now know as the SAS.

People still needed to be paid no matter how many staff we had left in these departments once the Marines had been shipped out. The armed forces pride themselves on the records they keep of every member of the forces, so in order for everything to function in their absence, we would all swap jobs every three to six months so we could step into any job at a moment's notice. It seemed to me to be such a simple and logical way to work and became the platform for the work I facilitated when working with teams in various organisations when I became a consultant.

After my contract with the Navy ended, I experienced a few civilian jobs, which showed me that not all businesses/organisations work the same way.

I briefly trained as a work study engineer with Johnson & Johnson, a position which fascinated and horrified me; people being watched and timed as they did their job so we, the engineers, could work out how they could work faster and more efficiently.

In time I became a full-time mum to my son and daughter.

As they were growing up, I trained as a 'listener' with the Citizens Advice Bureau. Our job was just that — to listen to people who came to us with a problem, to help and advise them on their next step. Their problems could be anything as simple as wanting to know bus times to presenting with more serious issues. It was our job to listen to them; to hear them out and to then refer them to a specialist counsellor if that was deemed appropriate.

Often just having someone to listen to them was all that people under stress needed.

I loved helping people so decided to train as a counsellor myself. I subsequently trained in marriage guidance counselling and later in Neuro-linguistic Programming (NLP) techniques.

After 17 years, my own marriage broke down and I found myself a solo mum with one teenager and one soon-to-be-teenager; a dog that ate everyone's shoes, and a battered old car that used more oil than petrol. I also had to face the fact that I had obsolete skills and a desperate financial need to get back into the workforce so I could pay the mortgage and feed us.

We were hit hard with the breakdown of our family and the financial challenges were enormous. It was particularly hard for us all to take on board these changed financial circumstances; difficulties which were compounded when I had no choice but to find full-time work in order to support us. So on top of the financial woes, they now had a mum they hardly saw.

The end result was two sad and confused kids who started displaying some pretty out-of-control behaviours as we all dealt with the pain and confusion of our new situation.

It was at this stage of my life that I heard about the concept of 'Toughlove', a movement which started in the USA to help families deal with solutions to unacceptable behaviours. Behaviours which, in some cases, were tearing their families apart.

The basic concept is that parents would get together weekly and talk through whatever issues they were struggling with, and by sharing their stories and hearing how other people had dealt with similar challenges, they were encouraged and supported to try different strategies. By having the backing and support of other parents, new people in the group would feel more confident to be able to deal with all manner of behaviours they felt totally unprepared for.

There were no groups in our area so to learn more about them I attended a public meeting and ended up joining forces with a school guidance counsellor to set up a group in our local area. It was a life-saver. I learned so much not only from the Toughlove philosophies, but also from other parents who had risked trying out scary new behaviours in order to stay sane during the painful teen years. These parents had succeeded in changing not only their kids' behaviours, but their own.

Meanwhile, on the job front, I took on a variety of low-skilled and low-paid jobs so I could pick up the skills required for a whole new computer age born in my years out of the workplace.

I subsequently became PA to a personnel manager; a man who saw things in me no-one else had ever seen and so despite my rusty skills, he trained me in all aspects of personnel management.

When he was eventually made redundant, I was offered the job as personnel officer — a seriously diminished version of his role and responsibilities, but a situation that presented me with a huge dilemma: my loyalty to a man who had trained me versus my desire to take on the role.

With his absolute encouragement I took the job.

I then had a fast-track career from personnel officer to personnel and industrial relations manager for a manufacturing company, to HR manager for a computer company and my ultimately terrifying decision to become an HR consultant in my own right.

As an HR consultant I've worked with businesses of all shapes and sizes, all colours and creeds. I specialised in working with high-performing teams sharing with them the strategies I'd learned while working with the Royal Marines and while learning the principles of work study.

I also worked in the areas of change management, performance management, succession planning and leadership. I've worked in areas as diverse as manufacturing and banking, technology and the health sector.

I trained as a 'profiler' to better help organisations recruit the right people for their culture. Understanding a person's personality via profiling also helped managers make more effective decisions with promotion and even with career direction and motivation. I talk about profiling in Chapter 7.

During the 30-plus years I worked in HR, I found it amazing that some of the techniques I had learned in counselling, marriage guidance and even Toughlove were totally transferable into the workplace. After all, there isn't much difference between a parent feeling powerless to deal with a teenager and a manager feeling powerless to know how to deal with a recalcitrant employee. And, similarly, there isn't a great deal of difference between an employee trying to get 'heard' by a manager and a teenager trying to put his or her point of view to a parent who grew up in a different era.

Parenting is a tough job; leadership is also a tough job. However, parenting and leadership come with certain responsibilities, and watching what is transpiring around the world has caused me such concern that I feel the absolute need to challenge what some people appear to think leadership is (unabridged power) and what it isn't (unabridged power).

> *'Pain travels through families until someone is ready to feel it.'*
> — Stephi Wagner

OTHER BOOKS BY THE AUTHOR

Shift Your But (Self-published 1999)

Finding the Square Root of a Banana (Self-published 2000)

Did I Really Employ You? (Published by Reed Publishing (NZ), 2004)

My Dear Franchisees (Self-published 2006)

Excellent Employment: Hiring the best people to help your business grow (Published by A & C Black, UK, 2007)

Mum's the Word by Vanessa Sunde, Kenina Court and Ann Andrews (Published by Phantom Publishing, 2007)

Lessons in Leadership: 50 Way to Avoid Falling into the 'Trump' Trap (Published by Moreau Publishing, 2017)

E-books

Dealing with Resistance to Change (2005)

It's Just a Numbers Game: How to set up a training/consulting business from scratch (2006)

Dealing with Poor Performance (2008)

Thousands of People Want to Do Business with You. Can They Find You? (2008)

Turning Ordinary Groups into Extra-ordinary Teams (2009)

12 Steps to Running Great Meetings (2009)

How to Write an E-book in 5 days (2009)

Warning: Unsafe Acts Can Cause Major Headaches (2012)

Bullies at Work (2014)

The 4 Stage Coaching Process (2015)

Fun and Games at Work (2016)

The 7 Tragic Ways Businesses Sabotage Their Own Success (2017)

Four Quadrant Leadership (2017)

REFERENCES

Preface

https://en.wikipedia.org/wiki/Anderson_Cooper

https://en.wikipedia.org/wiki/Wolf_Blitzer

https://en.wikipedia.org/wiki/Christiane_Amanpour

https://en.wikipedia.org/wiki/Fareed_Zakaria

https://en.wikipedia.org/wiki/David_Axelrod

https://en.wikipedia.org/wiki/Jake_Tapper

https://en.wikipedia.org/wiki/Don_Lemon

https://en.wikipedia.org/wiki/Carl_Bernstein

https://en.wikipedia.org/wiki/Bob_Woodward

Introduction

Lessons in Leadership: 50 ways to avoid falling into the 'Trump' trap

https://www.amazon.com/Lessons-Leadership-avoid-falling-Trump-ebook/dp/B077XJM1ML/

Chapter 1

https://en.wikipedia.org/wiki/Malala_Yousafzai

https://en.wikipedia.org/wiki/Mahatma_Gandhi

https://en.wikipedia.org/wiki/Abraham_Lincoln

https://en.wikipedia.org/wiki/Nelson_Mandela

https://en.wikipedia.org/wiki/John_F._Kennedy

https://en.wikipedia.org/wiki/Martin_Luther_King_Jr.

https://en.wikipedia.org/wiki/Mother_Teresa

https://en.wikipedia.org/wiki/List_of_whistleblowershttps://en.wikipedia.org/wiki/Rosa_Parks

https://en.wikipedia.org/wiki/Tarana_Burke

https://en.wikipedia.org/wiki/Harvey_Weinstein

https://en.wikipedia.org/wiki/Me_Too_movement

https://en.wikipedia.org/wiki/Time%27s_Up_(movement)

https://en.wikipedia.org/wiki/Alyssa_Milano

The Women's Timeline. https://www.mmu.ac.uk/equality-and-diversity/doc/gender-equality-timeline.pdf

Are women better leaders than men? by Jack Zenger and Joseph Folkman. Chapter 15, 2012.

https://hbr.org/2012/03/a-study-in-leadership-women-do

https://everipedia.org/wiki/jack-zenger/Joseph Folkman

https://www.ethics.org/

https://en.wikipedia.org/wiki/Hillary_Clinton

Chapter 2

https://en.wikipedia.org/wiki/Liberal_Party_(UK)

https://en.wikipedia.org/wiki/Social_Credit_Party_(New_Zealand)

https://en.wikipedia.org/wiki/Values_Party

https://en.wikipedia.org/wiki/Tony_Hayward

www.bbc.com/news/election-2017-40210957

A year after voting for Brexit, Britain's divided, and in uncharted waters. Timothy Gorton Ash. *The Guardian* 22.6.2017

https://www.theguardian.com/commentisfree/2017/jun/22/year-ago-britain-voted-leave-eu-worse-both-worlds

James Comey's fateful decision on Hillary Clinton's emails is slowly coming into focus. Aaron Blake. *The Washington Post.* 31.1.2017. https://www.washingtonpost.com/news/the-fix/wp/2018/01/31/james-comeys-fateful-decision-on-hillary-clintons-emails-is-slowly-coming-into-focus/

Johnson & Johnson ordered to pay record $417 million in lawsuit linking baby powder to cancer. Michael Balsamo. *The Star.* 21.8.2017. https://www.thestar.com/business/2017/08/21/johnson-johnson-ordered-to-pay-417-million-in-lawsuit-linking-baby-powder-to-cancer.html

https://en.wikipedia.org/wiki/Akio_Toyoda

Chapter 3

https://www.psychologytoday.com/us

https://www.merriam-webster.com/thesaurus/harasser

How to spot and stop manipulators. Preston Ni. MSBA. *Psychology Today*. 1.6.2014. https://www.psychologytoday.com/us/blog/communication-success/201406/how-spot-and-stop-manipulators

Bullying. *Employment New Zealand.* https://www.employment.govt.nz/resolving-problems/types-of-problems/bullying-harassment-and-discrimination/bullying/

Chamber of Commerce and Industry, WA. Which gender bullies more?

https://www.cciwa.com/about-us/news-and-media-statements/which-gender-bullies-more

Workplace Bullying Institute Report 2017. http://www.workplacebullying.org/wbiresearch/wbi-2017-survey/

The Cost of Bullying. Rachel Savage. Management Today. 16.11.2015.

https://www.managementtoday.co.uk/cost-workplace-bullying/article/1372942

https://en.wikipedia.org/wiki/Michael_Kranish

https://en.wikipedia.org/wiki/Marc_Fisher

https://en.wikipedia.org/wiki/Kim_Jong-un

https://en.wikipedia.org/wiki/Vladimir_Putin

https://en.wikipedia.org/wiki/Robert_Mueller

https://en.wikipedia.org/wiki/Michael_Avenatti

How Stormy Daniels and her brash lawyer cornered President Trump and Michael Cohen. Fredreka Schouten. *USA Today*. 11.4.2018. https://www.usatoday.com/story/news/politics/2018/04/10/stormy-daniels-michael-avenatti-donald-trump-michael-cohen-fbi-raid/503989002/

https://en.wikipedia.org/wiki/Stormy_Daniels

Chapter 4

https://en.wikipedia.org/wiki/Bernard_Montgomery

https://corporate.walmart.com/policies

https://en.wikipedia.org/wiki/Eric_Berne

https://en.wikipedia.org/wiki/Peter_Cook

https://en.wikipedia.org/wiki/Dudley_Moore

http://www.businessdictionary.com/definition/organizational-culture.html

'Choppergate' puts politicians' perks under scrutiny. Deborah Snow and James Robertson. *The Sydney Morning Herald*. 24.7.2015.

https://www.smh.com.au/politics/federal/choppergate-puts-politicians-perks-under-scrutiny-20150724-gijj5o.html

5 Outrageous CEO Spending Abuses And Perks. Linda McMaken. *Forbes*. 3.8.2011. https://www.forbes.com/sites/investopedia/2011/08/03/5-outrageous-ceo-spending-abuses-and-perks/#7c94a6ef3ae2

Waikato DHB chief executive quits. Aaron Leaman and Florence Kerr. *Stuff*. 5.10.2107. https://www.stuff.co.nz/national/health/97265223/waikato-dhb-to-learn-findings-into-absent-chief-executive

Oxfam: fresh claims that staff used prostitutes in Chad. Rebecca Ratcliffe and Ben Quinn. *The Observer*. 11.2.2018.

https://www.theguardian.com/world/2018/feb/10/oxfam-faces-allegations-staff-paid-prostitutes-in-chad

Where did 500 million dollars' worth of Red Cross donations go? Laura Nenitez-Ek. *The Grassroots Journal*. 29.1.2017

http://www.thegrassrootsjournal.org/single-post/2017/01/28/Where-did-500-million-dollars%E2%80%99-worth-of-Red-Cross-donations-go

Chapter 5

https://en.wikipedia.org/wiki/Jonathan_Chait

Here's the real reason everybody thought Trump would lose. Janathan Chait. *Daily Intelligencer*. 11.5. 2016.

http://nymag.com/intelligencer/2016/05/heres-the-real-reason-we-all-underrated-trump.html

Taking the pledge. https://www.bopdhb.govt.nz/patients-visitors/tauranga-hospital/

Meet the NHS whistle-blowers who exposed the truth. Patrick Sawyer and Laura Donnelly. *The Telegraph*. 11.2.2015.

http://www.telegraph.co.uk/news/health/news/11398148/The-NHS-whistle-blowers-who-spoke-out-for-patients.html

New Jersey agrees to settle trooper's harassment suit. Richard G. Jones. *The New York Times*. 2.10.2007.

https://www.nytimes.com/2007/10/02/nyregion/02lords.html

Citigroup Exec warned chairman of mortgage risk. *CBS News*. 7.4.2010

https://www.cbsnews.com/news/citigroup-exec-warned-chairman-of-mortgage-risk/

https://en.wikipedia.org/wiki/Karen_Silkwood

Christopher Wylie: Why I broke the Facebook data story – and what should happen now. Christopher Wylie. *The Guardian*. 7.4.2018.

https://en.wikipedia.org/wiki/Aleksandr_Kogan

A Cambridge Analytica Whistle-blower Claims That "Cheating" Swung the Brexit Vote. John Cassidy. *The New Yorker*. 28.3.2018.

https://www.newyorker.com/news/our-columnists/a-cambridge-analytica-whistleblower-claims-that-cheating-swung-the-brexit-vote

Enron: The fall of a Wall Street darling. Business Journal. 15.6.2015.

http://www.businessjournalng.com/enron-the-fall-of-a-wall-street-darling/

https://en.wikipedia.org/wiki/Wells_Fargo

https://en.wikipedia.org/wiki/Amtrak

https://en.wikipedia.org/wiki/GlaxoSmithKline

https://en.wikipedia.org/wiki/Pfizer

Chapter 6

A definition of politics https://goo.gl/su8xbN

https://www.amazon.com/Ethics-Politics-matters-difference-Globethics-net/dp/2940428212

https://en.wikipedia.org/wiki/Jacinda_Ardern

An '$11 billion hole': Expert analysis of Labour's fiscal plan after Steven Joyce called it a 'fiscal hole'. Audrey Young. *NZ Herald*. 5.9.2017

https://www.nzherald.co.nz/nz/news/article.cfm?c_id=1&objectid=11917655

Russian doping: Whistleblower Grigory Rodchenkov will testify but life under 'serious threat'

https://www.bbc.com/sport/winter-sports/42674331

Russia claims it could have been in the interests of Britain to poison Sergei Skripal. Lizzie Dearden. *The Independent*. 2.4.2018.

https://www.independent.co.uk/news/world/europe/sergei-skripal-latest-salisbury-poisoning-attack-russia-nerve-agent-sergei-lavrov-a8284766.html

Russia, in spy rift riposte, expels 59 diplomats from 23 countries. Andrew Osborn, Christian Lowe. *Reuters*. 31.3.2018.

https://www.reuters.com/article/us-britain-russia-diplomats/russia-in-spy-rift-riposte-expels-59-diplomats-from-23-countries-idUSKBN1H612R

https://en.wikipedia.org/wiki/Bashar_al-Assad

Dozens killed in apparent chemical weapons attack on civilians in Syria, rescue workers say. Louisa Lovelock and Erin Cunningham. *The Washington Post*. 8.4.2017. https://goo.gl/Hn3e7x

Trump is a master of diversionary tactics. Leonid Bershidsky. *The Chicago Tribune*. 26.1.2017.

http://www.chicagotribune.com/news/opinion/commentary/ct-trump-diversion-tactics-media-20170126-story.html

https://en.wikipedia.org/wiki/Leonid_Bershidsky

https://en.wikipedia.org/wiki/Kellyanne_Conway

https://en.wikipedia.org/wiki/Alternative_facts

https://en.wikipedia.org/wiki/Sean_Spicer

Study Finds That Having Power Can Make You Stupid. Frederick E. Allen. *Forbes*. 6.3.2012.

https://www.forbes.com/sites/frederickallen/2012/03/06/study-finds-that-having-power-can-make-you-stupid/#6c8c04c53288

Theresa May's decision to call a snap election may be the biggest political screw-up ever. Alex Shephard. *The New Republic*.

https://newrepublic.com/minutes/143230/theresa-mays-decision-call-snap-election-may-biggest-political-screw-up-ever

Hiroshima and Nagasaki death toll: http://www.aasc.ucla.edu/cab/200708230009.html

https://en.wikipedia.org/wiki/Mao_Zedong

https://en.wikipedia.org/wiki/Douglas_MacArthur

https://en.wikipedia.org/wiki/Robert_McNamara

https://en.wikipedia.org/wiki/Saddam_Hussein

The cost of war in Iraq. National Priorities Project

https://www.nationalpriorities.org/campaigns/cost-war-iraq/

Karin Lang. 'What Happened' by Hillary Clinton https://goo.gl/ay9nBb

https://en.wikipedia.org/wiki/James_Comey

https://en.wikipedia.org/wiki/Raymond_J._Donovan

https://en.wikipedia.org/wiki/Kevin_McCarthy_(California_politician)

Chapter 7

https://en.wikipedia.org/wiki/Hippocrates

https://en.wikipedia.org/wiki/Four_temperaments

https://www.amazon.com/Trumps-Brain-Profile-Predicting-Presidency-ebook/dp/B01N5RCDH3

Narcissistic Personality Disorder.

https://www.psychologytoday.com/conditions/narcissistic-personality-disorder

The toxic effect of a narcissistic leader. Brian Amble. 9.4.2010.

http://www.management-issues.com/news/5912/the-toxic-effect-of-a-narcissistic-leader/

At Yale, Psychiatrists Cite Their 'Duty to Warn' About an Unfit President. Gail Sheehy. *Intelligencer*. 23.4.2017.

http://nymag.com/daily/intelligencer/2017/04/yale-psychiatrists-cite-duty-to-warn-about-unfit-president.html

https://en.wikipedia.org/wiki/Goldwater_rule

http://www.johngartner.com/about.php

https://en.wikipedia.org/wiki/Bandy_X._Lee

https://en.wikipedia.org/wiki/Robert_Jay_Lifton

Baltimore psychologist heads effort to 'warn' about Trump's mental health. John Fritze. *The Baltimore Sun*. 24.9.2017.

http://www.baltimoresun.com/news/maryland/politics/bs-md-gartner-duty-to-warn-20170918-story.html

https://en.wikipedia.org/wiki/Judith_Lewis_Herman

https://en.wikipedia.org/wiki/James_Gilligan

Chapter 8

https://en.wikipedia.org/wiki/Electoral_College_(United_States)

Anthony Scaramucci tears into 'bad dude' Trump chief of staff John Kelly. Jennifer Jacobs. *Stuff*. 2.3.2018. https://www.stuff.co.nz/world/americas/101909541/anthony-scaramucci-tears-into-bad-dude-trump-chief-of-staff-john-kelly

Trump asking John Kelly for help in pushing Ivanka, Kushner out of White House. Veronika Stracqualursi. NYT. 2.3.2018.

https://edition.cnn.com/2018/03/02/politics/trump-john-kelly-ivanka/index.html

https://en.wikipedia.org/wiki/Enrique_Pe%C3%B1a_Nieto

https://en.wikipedia.org/wiki/Deferred_Action_for_Childhood_Arrivals

https://en.wikipedia.org/wiki/Michael_Wolff_(journalist)

16 Things You Didn't Know About Donald Trump's Father, Fred. Kaitlin Menza. *Town & Country*. 6.4.2017.

https://www.townandcountrymag.com/society/money-and-power/g9229257/fred-trump-facts/

https://en.wikipedia.org/wiki/Ku_Klux_Klan

Who Are Trump's Parents? Here's What We Can Learn From The President's Family History. Andrea Frazier. *Romper*. 15.8.2017. https://www.romper.com/p/who-are-trumps-parents-heres-what-we-can-learn-from-the-presidents-family-history-76523

Donald Trump's Immigrant Mother. Mary Pilon. *The New Yorker*. 24.6.2016.

https://www.newyorker.com/news/news-desk/donald-trumps-immigrant-mother

The Trump effect: An update. Rosemary K.M. Sword and Philip Zimbardo PhD. *Psychology Today*. 30.1.2018.

https://www.psychologytoday.com/us/blog/the-time-cure/201801/the-trump-effect-update

https://www.hsph.harvard.edu/david-williams/

Could the stress of a Trump presidency Make America Sick? Maggie Fox. *NBC News*. 8.6.2017.

https://www.nbcnews.com/health/health-news/could-stress-trump-presidency-make-americans-sick-n769441

In Washington Pizzeria Attack, Fake News Brought Real Guns. Cecilia Kang and Adam Goldman. *The New York Times*. 5.12.2016.

https://www.nytimes.com/2016/12/05/business/media/comet-ping-pong-pizza-shooting-fake-news-consequences.html

Video interview. NBC Nightly News Anchor Lester Holt interviews Donald Trump.

https://en.wikipedia.org/wiki/Lester_Holt

Why we lie: The science behind our deceptive ways. Yudhijit Bhattacharjee. *National Geographic*. June 2017.

https://www.nationalgeographic.com/magazine/2017/06/lying-hoax-false-fibs-science/

https://www.msnbc.com/brian-williams/watch/trump-connects-comey-firing-to-russia-questions-in-nbc-interview-942122051703

https://brionyswire.com/

https://me.me/i/a-recent-study-led-by-briony-swire-thompson-a-doctoral-candidate-14764061

https://en.wikipedia.org/wiki/David_J._Ley

6 reasons people lie when they don't need to. David J. Ley PhD. *Psychology Today*. 23.1.2017.

https://www.psychologytoday.com/us/blog/women-who-stray/201701/6-reasons-people-lie-when-they-don-t-need

Fact Check: Has Trump declared bankruptcy four times or six times? Michelle Lee. *The Washington Post*. 27.9.2016. https://goo.gl/DqkYYc

Study finds Trump voters believe Trump is authentic, even if he appears to lie. Caroline Tanner. *USA Today*. 2.5.2018. https://www.usatoday.com/story/news/politics/onpolitics/2018/05/02/trump-supporters-were-more-enthusiastic-their-support-him-candidate-extent-they-justified-trumps-lie/573371002/

The authentic appeal of the lying demagogue: Proclaiming the deeper truth about political illegitimacy. Oliver Hahl, Minjae Kim, Ezra W. Zuckerman Sivan. *American Sociological Review*. 10.1.2018. http://journals.sagepub.com/doi/abs/10.1177/0003122417749632

https://en.wikipedia.org/wiki/American_Sociological_Review

Trump Has Called Climate Change a Chinese Hoax. Beijing Says It Is Anything But. Edward Wong. *The New York Times*. 18.11.2016. https://www.nytimes.com/2016/11/19/world/asia/china-trump-climate-change.html

Journalists banned from entering EPA meeting on contaminated drinking water. Mythili Sampathkumar. *Independent*. 22.5.2018.

https://www.independent.co.uk/news/world/americas/us-politics/epa-meeting-journalists-banned-contaminated-water-scott-pruitt-a8364111.html

https://en.wikipedia.org/wiki/Scott_Pruitt

https://en.wikipedia.org/wiki/Rex_Tillerson

https://en.wikipedia.org/wiki/Teresa_Manning

https://en.wikipedia.org/wiki/Lynne_Patton

https://en.wikipedia.org/wiki/Keith_Schiller

https://en.wikipedia.org/wiki/Jared_Kushner

Ronny Jackson: top veterans job for doctor who praised Trump's 'incredible genes'

The Guardian. 29.3.2018. https://www.theguardian.com/us-news/2018/mar/29/ronny-jackson-doctor-trump-veterans-affairs

U.S. Needs New FAA Head, Trump Generously Offers His Personal Pilot. Margaret Hartmann. *Intelligencer*. http://nymag.com/daily/intelligencer/2018/02/u-s-needs-new-faa-head-trump-offers-his-personal-pilot.html

Trump's Heartless Transgender Military Ban Gets a Second Shot. *The New York Times*. 28.3.2018. https://www.nytimes.com/2018/03/28/opinion/trump-transgender-military-ban.html

https://en.wikipedia.org/wiki/Jim_Mattis

https://www.americanactionforum.org/experts/ben-gitis/

Mass deportations would cost families US billions: Study. Patricia Guadalup. *NBC News*. 1.2.2017.

https://www.nbcnews.com/news/latino/mass-deportation-would-cost-families-u-s-billions-study-n715236

Losing Immigrant Workers on Dairy Farms Would Nearly Double Retail Milk Prices

https://www.agweb.com/article/losing-immigrant-workers-on-dairy-farms-would-nearly-double-retail-milk-prices-naa-news-release/

The Americans Left Behind by Deportation. Karla Cornejo Villavicencio. *The New York Times*. 28.2.2018. https://www.nytimes.com/2018/02/28/opinion/american-families-immigrants-deportation.html

Hundreds of Immigrant Children Have Been Taken From Parents at U.S. Border. Caitlin Dickerson. *The New York Times*. 20.4.2018.

https://www.nytimes.com/2018/04/20/us/immigrant-children-separation-ice.html

https://www.osha.gov/

OSHA won't tell you who died in the work-place but we will. 28.8.2017.

http://www.allgov.com/officials/barab-jordan?officialid=28933

Here's What You Need to Know About Donald Trump's Lawsuits: he's been sued more than 100 times since his inauguration. Caroline Halleman. *Town & Country*. 29.8.2017.

https://www.townandcountrymag.com/society/politics/a9962852/lawsuits-against-donald-trump/

It was a bad day in court for Donald Trump's efforts to silence women. Anna North. *Vox*. 20.3.2018.

https://www.vox.com/policy-and-politics/2018/3/20/17144160/karen-mcdougal-playboy-model-donald-trump-summer-zervos-lawsuit

Trump picks the 'Fake News Washington Post' as the newest target in his war against Amazon and Jeff Bezos. Bob Bryan. *The Washington Post*. 5.4.2018.
https://www.businessinsider.com.au/trump-amazon-washington-post-war-with-jeff-bezos-2018-4

Amazon falls again after Trump tweets it's a 'scam' costing the post office 'billions'. Fred Imbert. *CNBC*. 2.4.2018.

https://www.cnbc.com/2018/04/02/amazon-is-under-pressure-again-after-trump-tweets-its-a-scam-costing-the-post-office-billions.html

Trump will slap 10% tariffs on $200 billion in Chinese goods — and they will go to 25% at year-end. Jacob Pramuk. *CNBC*. 18.9.2018.

https://www.cnbc.com/2018/09/17/trump-puts-new-tariffs-on-china-as-trade-war-escalates.html

https://en.wikipedia.org/wiki/It%27s_the_economy,_stupid

https://ustr.gov/trade-agreements/free-trade-agreements/north-american-free-trade-agreement-nafta

https://en.wikipedia.org/wiki/Trans-Pacific_Partnership

God Syndrome. Nassir Ghaemi. MD. MPH. *Psychology Today*. 20.10.2008.

https://www.psychologytoday.com/us/blog/mood-swings/200810/god-syndrome

Why we lie: The science behind our deceptive ways. Yudhijit Bhattacharjee. *National Geographic*. June 2017.

https://www.nationalgeographic.com/magazine/2017/06/lying-hoax-false-fibs-science/

https://www.nih.gov/

https://en.wikipedia.org/wiki/Colleen_Kollar-Kotelly

https://www.linkedin.com/in/bgitis/

https://www.americanactionforum.org/

http://www.nmpf.org/about-nmpf

http://www.imf.org/external/index.htm

https://en.wikipedia.org/wiki/Lawrence_Summers

Trump thinks he has nothing to lose in a trade war with China. He's wrong. Zeeshan Aleem. *Vox*. 5.4.2018.

https://www.vox.com/2018/4/4/17196972/trump-china-trade-war-tariffs

https://en.wikipedia.org/wiki/Steve_Bannon

https://en.wikipedia.org/wiki/Barack_Obama_citizenship_conspiracy_theories

We thought the Nazi threat was dead. But Donald Trump has revived it. Jonathan Freedland. *The Guardian*. 25.8.2017.

https://www.theguardian.com/commentisfree/2017/aug/25/donald-trump-nazis-far-right-charlottesville

https://en.wikipedia.org/wiki/Code_talker

https://en.wikipedia.org/wiki/Elizabeth_Warren

https://en.wikipedia.org/wiki/Pocahontas

11 Warning Signs of Gaslighting. Stephanie A. Sarkis. PhD. *Psychology Today*. 22.1.2017.

https://www.psychologytoday.com/us/blog/here-there-and-everywhere/201701/11-warning-signs-gaslighting

Trump reportedly wants an immediate pull-out from Syria but military officials are fighting back. Malcolm Lee and Josh Lederman. *Business Insider*. 5.4.2018.

http://www.businessinsider.com/trump-syria-us-troops-withdraw-2018-4/

'No more DACA deal,' Trump says as he threatens to 'stop' NAFTA if Mexico doesn't better secure border. Philip Rucker and David Weigal. *The Washington Post*. 2.4.2018.

https://www.washingtonpost.com/news/post-politics/wp/2018/04/01/deal-on-daca-no-more-trump-says/

Chapter 9

https://en.wikipedia.org/wiki/Aleksandr_Kogan

https://en.wikipedia.org/wiki/SCL_Group

Facebook failed to protect 30 million users from having their data harvested by Trump campaign affiliate. Mattathias Schwartz. *The Intercept*. 31.3.2017.

https://theintercept.com/2017/03/30/facebook-failed-to-protect-30-million-users-from-having-their-data-harvested-by-trump-campaign-affiliate/

https://en.wikipedia.org/wiki/Mark_Zuckerberg

Alleged Russian political meddling documented in 27 countries since 2004. Oren Dorell. USA Today. 7.9.2017.

https://www.usatoday.com/story/news/world/2017/09/07/alleged-russian-political-meddling-documented-27-countries-since-2004/619056001/

Zuckerberg barely talked about Facebook's biggest global problem. Adam Taylor. The Washington Post. 13.4.2018

https://www.washingtonpost.com/news/worldviews/wp/2018/04/13/zuckerberg-barely-talked-about-facebooks-biggest-global-problem/

https://en.wikipedia.org/wiki/Sheryl_Sandberg

https://en.wikipedia.org/wiki/Roger_McNamee

https://en.wikipedia.org/wiki/Steve_Wozniak

Facebook faces exodus as businesses call time. Adam Zuchetti. *My Business*. 23.4.2018.

https://www.mybusiness.com.au/technology/4229-facebook-exodus-as-businesses-call-time

Chapter 10

https://en.wikipedia.org/wiki/Malcolm_X

https://en.wikipedia.org/wiki/Sam_Johnson_(activist)

https://en.wikipedia.org/wiki/Emmanuel_Macron

https://en.wikipedia.org/wiki/Matteo_Fiorini

https://en.wikipedia.org/wiki/J%C3%BCri_Ratas

https://en.wikipedia.org/wiki/Leo_Varadkar

https://en.wikipedia.org/wiki/Jigme_Khesar_Namgyel_Wangchuck

https://en.wikipedia.org/wiki/Chl%C3%B6e_Swarbrick

https://en.wikipedia.org/wiki/John_McCallum

https://www.ipsos.com/en

https://en.wikipedia.org/wiki/Compulsory_voting

https://en.wikipedia.org/wiki/George_Stephanopoulos

https://en.wikipedia.org/wiki/Kenneth_Frazier

https://en.wikipedia.org/wiki/John_D._Feeley

US ambassador to Panama resigns; says cannot serve Trump. *Reuters*. 13.1.2018.

https://www.reuters.com/article/us-usa-diplomacy-panama/u-s-ambassador-to-panama-resigns-says-cannot-serve-trump-idUSKBN1F1227

Chapter 11

https://en.wikipedia.org/wiki/Iyanla_Vanzant

https://en.wikipedia.org/wiki/John_McCain

https://en.wikipedia.org/wiki/Michelle_Obama

https://en.wikipedia.org/wiki/Donald_Rumsfeld

Why John McCain killed Obamacare repeal – again. Ryan Lizza. *The New Yorker*. 22.9.2017.

https://www.newyorker.com/news/ryan-lizza/why-john-mccain-killed-obamacare-repealagain

https://en.wikipedia.org/wiki/David_Lloyd_George

How Winston Churchill lost the 1945 election. *The Conversation*. 21.1.2015.

https://theconversation.com/how-winston-churchill-lost-the-1945-election-36411

https://en.wikipedia.org/wiki/Paul_Addison

https://en.wikipedia.org/wiki/Labour_Party_(UK)

https://en.wikipedia.org/wiki/Battle_of_Dunkirk

https://en.wikipedia.org/wiki/Richard_Nixon

https://en.wikipedia.org/wiki/Watergate_scandal

https://en.wikipedia.org/wiki/Jimmy_Carter

Obama's presidential centre will focus on grassroots activism and developing new leaders. Max de Haldevang. *Quartz*. 21.1.2017.

https://qz.com/890473/obamas-presidential-center-will-focus-on-grassroots-activism-and-developing-new-leaders/

Addressing homelessness. Jason Johnson. Interim Director Seattle Human Services

https://www.seattle.gov/humanservices/about-us/initiatives/addressing-homelessness

Amazon pausing Seattle construction because of business tax proposal. Sarah Anne Lloyd. Curbed. 2.5.2018 https://seattle.curbed.com/2018/5/2/17312340/amazon-head-tax-construction-halt

Philanthropy 50. *The Chronicle of Philanthropy.*

https://www.philanthropy.com/interactives/philanthropy-50

A commitment to philanthropy. The Giving Pledge. https://givingpledge.org/

https://en.wikipedia.org/wiki/World_Giving_Index

Chapter 12

The case against corporate short termism. Tim Koller, James Manyika and Sree Ramaswamy. 4.8.2017.

https://www.mckinsey.com/mgi/overview/in-the-news/the-case-against-corporate-short-termism

https://www.oann.com/tag/corporate-horizon-index/

https://en.wikipedia.org/wiki/DDT

https://en.wikipedia.org/wiki/Catch_share

http://therevolutionmovie.com/index.php/open-your-eyes/overfishing/solutions/

China's appetite pushes fisheries to the brink. Andrew Jacobs. *The New York Times*. 30.4.2017.

https://www.nytimes.com/2017/04/30/world/asia/chinas-appetite-pushes-fisheries-to-the-brink.html

Why Cape Town is running out of water, and who's next. Craig Welch. *National Geographic*. 5.3.2018.

https://news.nationalgeographic.com/2018/02/cape-town-running-out-of-water-drought-taps-shutoff-other-cities/

Clear water, blue skies: China's environment in the new century. The World Bank.

http://documents.worldbank.org/curated/en/944011468743999953/Clear-water-blue-skies-Chinas-environment-in-the-new-century

UN Report: World Faces 40% Water Shortfall by 2030. *VOA News*. 22.3.2015.

https://www.voanews.com/a/un-report-world-faces-40-percent-water-shortfall-by-2030/2690205.html

https://en.wikipedia.org/wiki/Pollution_of_the_Ganges

https://en.wikipedia.org/wiki/Pasig_River

https://en.wikipedia.org/wiki/Citarum_River

https://en.wikipedia.org/wiki/Flint_water_crisis

https://en.wikipedia.org/wiki/Mona_Hanna-Attisha

Trump signs bill undoing Obama coal mining rule. Devin Henry. *The Hill.* 16.2.2017.

https://thehill.com/policy/energy-environment/319938-trump-signs-bill-undoing-obama-coal-mining-rule

Mining the mountains. John McQuaid. *Smithsonian Magazine*. January 2009.

https://www.smithsonianmag.com/science-nature/mining-the-mountains-130454620/

https://www.epa.govt.nz/

Long-Term Costs Of Fracking Are Staggering. Jane Dale Own. *Think Progress*. 19.3.2013.

https://thinkprogress.org/long-term-costs-of-fracking-are-staggering-16b1160f98c6/

Do other countries use fracking? Brad Plumer. *Vox*. 30.7.2015.

https://www.vox.com/cards/fracking/do-other-countries-use-fracking

https://www.britannica.com/biography/J-David-Hughes

List of worldwide fracking country bans. *ASMAA*. 30.4.2018.

http://www.asmaa-algarve.org/en/blog/fracking/list-of-worldwide-fracking-country-bans

http://www.eco.org.nz/key-issues/mining/fracking.html

Fracking related earthquakes. *Earthworks*. https://goo.gl/GkFTBm

Air Pollution in China: Real-time Air Quality Index Visual Map. *Air Quality Index*.

http://aqicn.org/map/china/

What it's like to live in the world's most polluted city. Melody Rowell. *National Geographic*. 26.4.2016.

https://news.nationalgeographic.com/2016/04/160425-new-delhi-most-polluted-city-matthieu-paley/

Here are some of the world's worst cities for air quality. Katherine Kornei. *Science Magazine*. 21.3.2017.

http://www.sciencemag.org/news/2017/03/here-are-some-world-s-worst-cities-air-quality

These 5 countries account for 60% of plastic pollution in oceans. Lorraine Chow. *EcoWatch*. 15.10.2015.

https://www.ecowatch.com/these-5-countries-account-for-60-of-plastic-pollution-in-oceans-1882107531.html

48 million people in China lack sufficient drinking water.

http://factsanddetails.com/china/cat13/sub85/item317.html

High levels of plastic and debris found in waters off Antarctica. Joseph Stromberg. *Smithsonian*. 3.10.2012.

https://www.smithsonianmag.com/science-nature/high-levels-of-plastic-and-debris-found-in-waters-off-of-antarctica-58721328/

Long before sinking Roy Moore's candidacy, black women in Alabama were a force for change. DeNeen L. Brown. *The Washington Post*. 16.12.2017.

https://www.washingtonpost.com/news/retropolis/wp/2017/12/16/long-before-sinking-roy-moores-candidacy-black-women-in-alabama-have-been-a-force/

US politician who mocked Women's March defeated by woman he inspired to run. Paul Owen. *The Guardian*. 8.11.2017.

https://www.theguardian.com/us-news/2017/nov/08/new-jersey-womens-march-joke-candidate-beaten

Trans woman Danica Roem beats 'chief homophobe' Bob Marshall in historic Virginia race. Brittany Levine Beckman. AOL. 7.11.2017.

https://www.aol.com/article/news/2017/11/08/trans-woman-danica-roem-beats-chief-homophobe-bob-marshall-in-historic-virginia-race/23270498/

https://en.wikipedia.org/wiki/Nikki_Haley

Nikki Haley: women who accuse Trump of sexual misconduct 'should be heard'. Martin Pengelly. *The Guardian*. 10.12.2017.

https://www.theguardian.com/us-news/2017/dec/10/nikki-haley-donald-trump-accusers-should-be-heard

https://medium.com/transequalitynow/fight-back-and-help-defeat-anti-transgender-state-legislation-25f75437a955

http://documents.worldbank.org/curated/en/944011468743999953/Clear-water-blue-skies-Chinas-environment-in-the-new-century

The 20 most environmentally-friendly countries. Oliver Smith. *The Telegraph*. 22.4.2017.

http://www.telegraph.co.uk/travel/maps-and-graphics/most-and-least-environmentally-friendly-countries/

Florida Legislators OK Plan to Dump Sewage Into Drinking-Water Aquifers. *USA Breaking News*. 12.3.2018.

https://www.usabreakingnews.net/2018/03/florida-legislators-ok-plan-to-dump-sewage-into-drinking-water-aquifers/

The USA *is* going fossil free. *Fossil Free USA*. https://gofossilfree.org/usa/

Oceans release DDT from decades ago. Richard A. Lovett. *Nature*. 7.1.2010.

http://www.nature.com/news/2010/100107/full/news.2010.4.html

The collapse of the Canadian Newfoundland cod fishery. Greenpeace. 8.5.2009.

https://www.greenpeace.org/archive-international/en/

campaigns/oceans/seafood/understanding-the-problem/overfishing-history/cod-fishery-canadian/

https://en.wikipedia.org/wiki/Richard_A._Lovett

Population Growth 1939 to 2009. L.J. Furman. *Popular Logistics*. 3.10.2009.

http://popularlogistics.com/2009/10/population-growth-1939-to-2009/

The world population clock. https://goo.gl/642XCN

What are the 10 biggest global challenges? Rosamund Hutt. World Economic Forum. 21.1.2016.

https://www.weforum.org/agenda/2016/01/what-are-the-10-biggest-global-challenges/

India poised to join China as global leaders in renewables: Report. *IANS. Economic Times*. 22.5.2018.

https://economictimes.indiatimes.com/industry/energy/power/india-poised-to-join-china-as-global-leaders-in-renewables-report/articleshow/64269867.cms

Chapter 13

Roseanne TV show CANCELLED after Barr compared Obama White House adviser to ape on Twitter. F. Thistlethwaite. *Express*. 29.5.2018.

https://www.express.co.uk/showbiz/tv-radio/966658/Roseanne-TV-show-cancelled-ABC-Obama-White-House-Valerie-Jarrett

https://en.wikipedia.org/wiki/Anita_Roddick

https://en.wikipedia.org/wiki/2017_Women%27s_March

Women's Suffrage Movement. HistoryNet.

http://www.historynet.com/womens-suffrage-movement

https://en.wikipedia.org/wiki/Married_Women%27s_Property_Act_1882

Women and the vote. New Zealand History.

https://nzhistory.govt.nz/politics/womens-suffrage

https://en.wikipedia.org/wiki/Sex_Discrimination_Act

https://www.parliament.uk/about/living-heritage/transformingsociety/private-lives/yourcountry/overview/conscriptionww2/

https://www.nhs.uk/using-the-nhs/about-the-nhs/history-of-the-nhs/the-nhs-from-1948-to-1959/

https://en.wikipedia.org/wiki/Ford_sewing_machinists_strike_of_1968

https://en.wikipedia.org/wiki/America_Ferrera

https://en.wikipedia.org/wiki/Ashley_Judd

#MeToo and Time's Up Founders Explain the Difference Between the 2 Movements — And How They're Alike. Alix Langone. *Time*. 22.3.2018.

http://time.com/5189945/whats-the-difference-between-the-metoo-and-times-up-movements/

https://en.wikipedia.org/wiki/Time%27s_Up_(movement)

Time's up legal defense fund. National Women's Law Centre.

https://nwlc.org/times-up-legal-defense-fund/

https://en.wikipedia.org/wiki/Doug_Jones_(politician)

How Doug Jones beat Roy Moore. Amy Davidson Sorkin. *The New Yorker*. 13.12.2017.

https://www.newyorker.com/news/daily-comment/how-doug-jones-beat-roy-moore

US politician who mocked Women's March defeated by woman he inspired to run. Paul Owen. *The Guardian*. 8.11.2017.

https://www.theguardian.com/us-news/2017/nov/08/new-jersey-womens-march-joke-candidate-beaten

https://en.wikipedia.org/wiki/Bob_Marshall_(Virginia_politician)

https://en.wikipedia.org/wiki/Larry_Kudlow

http://time.com/5245537/nikki-haley-i-dont-get-confused-larry-kudlow-spat/

https://en.wikipedia.org/wiki/Colin_Kaepernick

https://en.wikipedia.org/wiki/Jeff_Flake

Full Transcript: Jeff Flake's Speech on the Senate Floor. *The New York Times*. 24.10.2017.

https://www.nytimes.com/2017/10/24/us/politics/jeff-flake-transcript-senate-speech.html

Full list of 233 firms named and shamed for failing to pay the minimum wage. Mark Ellis and Mikey Smith. *Mirror*. 20.8.2017.

https://www.mirror.co.uk/news/politics/full-list-233-firms-named-10999800

Domino's, KFC and Gloria Jean's 'named and shamed' for unsafe food practices — so is YOUR local on the list?

http://www.dailymail.co.uk/news/article-4705816/Domino-s-food-outlets-NSW-shame-list.html

EU blacklist names 17 tax havens and puts Caymans and Jersey on notice. Daniel Boffey. *The Guardian*. 5.12.17.

https://www.theguardian.com/business/2017/dec/05/eu-blacklist-names-17-tax-havens-and-puts-caymans-and-jersey-on-notice

https://en.wikipedia.org/wiki/Jim_Yong_Kim

Glasgow University becomes the first UK University to divest from fossil fuel industry. *University News*. 8.10.2014.

https://www.gla.ac.uk/news/archiveofnews/2014/october/headline_364008_en.html

Fossil fuel divestment: a brief history. Adam Vaughan. *The Guardian*. 8.10.2014.

https://www.theguardian.com/environment/2014/oct/08/fossil-fuel-divestment-a-brief-history

https://en.wikipedia.org/wiki/Bill_McKibben

China releases 2020 action plan for air pollution. Feng Hao. *China Dialogue*. 6.7.2018.

https://www.chinadialogue.net/article/show/single/en/10711-China-releases-2-2-action-plan-for-air-pollution

https://en.wikipedia.org/wiki/Bhadla_Solar_Park

Germany considering free public transport to take on air pollution. Rebecca Staudenmaier. *DW*. 13.2.2018.

http://www.dw.com/en/germany-considering-free-public-transportation-to-take-on-air-pollution/a-42574053

https://en.wikipedia.org/wiki/Finland_National_Renewable_Energy_Action_Plan

Why Trump just killed a rule restricting coal companies from dumping waste in streams. Brad Plumer. *Vox*. 16.2.2017.

https://www.vox.com/2017/2/2/14488448/stream-protection-rule

Climate change: Michael Bloomberg pledges $4.5m for Paris deal. *BBC News*. 23.4.2018.

https://www.bbc.com/news/world-us-canada-43860590

https://en.wikipedia.org/wiki/Michael_Bloomberg

Sweden's recycling is so revolutionary the country has run out of rubbish. Hazel Sheffield. *Independent*. 8.12.2016.

https://www.independent.co.uk/environment/sweden-s-recycling-is-so-revolutionary-the-country-has-run-out-of-rubbish-a7462976.html

Dutch prisons are closing because the country is so safe. Chris Weller. *Business Insider*. 31.5.2017.

https://www.independent.co.uk/news/world/europe/dutch-prisons-are-closing-because-the-country-is-so-safe-a7765521.html

A self-made billionaire is giving away his fortune to clean up the oceans. David Reid. CNBC. 18.5.2017.

https://www.cnbc.com/2017/05/18/a-billionaire-is-giving-his-fortune-away-to-clean-up-oceans.html

https://en.wikipedia.org/wiki/Boyan_Slat

https://www.ted.com/about/programs-initiatives/tedx-program

First-ever ocean plastic cleaner will tackle Great Pacific Garbage Patch. Saquib Shah. *The New York Post*. 23.4.2018.

https://nypost.com/2018/04/23/first-ever-ocean-plastic-cleaner-will-tackle-great-pacific-garbage-patch/

Legendary Roger Federer spends whopping $13.5m to open 81 schools in Africa. Chaithanya. *The Youth*. 30.11.2017.

http://theyouth.in/2017/11/30/legendary-roger-federer-spends-whopping-13-5m-to-open-81-schools-in-africa/

'Youthquake' named 2017 word of the year by Oxford Dictionaries. Sian Cain. *The Guardian*. 15.12.2017.

https://www.theguardian.com/books/2017/dec/15/youthquake-named-2017-word-of-the-year-by-oxford-dictionaries

https://en.wikipedia.org/wiki/National_Rifle_Association

Parkland teens are calling out critics on social media. Jen Kirby. *Vox*. 26.2.2018.

https://www.vox.com/2018/2/26/17054408/parkland-shooting-activist-teens-gun-control

Young People Keep Marching After Parkland, This Time to Register to Vote. Michael Tackett and Rachel Shorey. *The New York Times*. 20.3.2018.

https://en.wikipedia.org/wiki/J._K._Rowling

https://en.wikipedia.org/wiki/Paris_Agreement

The history of Earth Day

https://www.earthday.org/about/the-history-of-earth-day/

https://en.wikipedia.org/wiki/John_McConnell_(peace_activist)

https://en.wikipedia.org/wiki/Gaylord_Nelson

Chapter 14

https://en.wikipedia.org/wiki/Alvin_Toffler

http://www.lawrencewright.com/

https://en.wikipedia.org/wiki/David_Hogg_(activist)

https://www.nytimes.com/2018/05/20/us/politics/young-voters-registration-parkland.html

Florida students take on NRA, set eyes on midterm elections. Andrew Hay. *Reuters*. 25.2.2018.

https://www.reuters.com/article/us-usa-guns-students/florida-students-take-on-nra-set-eyes-on-midterm-elections-idUSKCN1G80GT

Global Shapers Survey. Annual Survey. 2017.

http://shaperssurvey2017.org/static/data/WEF_GSC_Annual_Survey_2017.pdf

https://www.weforum.org/

https://en.wikipedia.org/wiki/Elon_Musk

https://www.gartner.com/newsroom/id/3837763

http://www.bbc.com/news/world-us-canada-42170100

https://en.wikipedia.org/wiki/Kathleen_Wynne

Canadian province trials basic income for thousands of residents. Benjamin Kentish. *Independent*. 29.11.2017.

https://www.independent.co.uk/news/world/americas/canada-universal-basic-income-ontario-trial-citizens-residents-poverty-unemployment-benefits-a8082576.html

Free cash to fight income inequality? California City is first in US to try. Peter S. Goodman. *The New York Times*. 30.5.2018.

https://www.nytimes.com/2018/05/30/business/stockton-basic-income.html

https://en.wikipedia.org/wiki/Albert_Camus

https://en.wikipedia.org/wiki/Genghis_Khan#Death_and_burial

https://en.wikipedia.org/wiki/Joseph_Stalin

https://en.wikipedia.org/wiki/Pol_Pot

https://en.wikipedia.org/wiki/Idi_Amin

https://en.wikipedia.org/wiki/Robert_Mugabe

https://www.historytoday.com/richard-cavendish/death-joseph-stalin

Pol Pot overthrown. *History*. 1979. https://www.history.com/this-day-in-history/pol-pot-overthrown

Idi Amin overthrown. *History*. 1979. https://www.history.com/this-day-in-history/idi-amin-overthrown

Mugabe resigns under military pressure after 37 years as Zimbabwe's leader. Kevin Sieff. *The Washington Post*. 21.11.2017. https://goo.gl/KP2gtj

https://www.thetimes.co.uk/article/zimbabwe-s-exiled-white-farmers-get-lifeline-to-return-gcgg0n333

https://en.wikipedia.org/wiki/Emmerson_Mnangagwa

https://en.wikipedia.org/wiki/Max_Boot

https://www.theguardian.com/profile/peterbeaumont

https://www.theguardian.com/world/2011/mar/02/protests-how-dictators-fall

Chapter 15

https://en.wikipedia.org/wiki/Charles_de_Gaulle

http://www.massey.ac.nz/massey/about-massey/news/article.cfm?mnarticle_uuid=9AA7647B-0864-1798-6495-CC7CA330FCAF

http://www.dictionary.com/browse/democracy

https://en.wikipedia.org/wiki/Kia_kaha

https://en.wikipedia.org/wiki/M%C4%81ori_people

www.ingramcontent.com/pod-product-compliance
Lightning Source LLC
Chambersburg PA
CBHW072104040426
42334CB00042B/2307

* 9 7 8 0 9 5 8 2 6 3 4 7 4 *